HOMES FOR PEOPLE:

COUNCIL HOUSING AND URBAN RENEWAL IN BIRMINGHAM, 1849 – 1999

HOMES FOR PEOPLE:

COUNCIL HOUSING AND URBAN RENEWAL IN BIRMINGHAM, 1849 – 1999

Carl Chinn

First published in 1999 by
Brewin Books, Studley, Warwickshire B80 7LG

Second Impression September 1999
Third Impression February 2001
Fourth Impression November 2004

British Library Cataloguing in Publication Data
A catalogue record for this book is available from
The British Library

ISBN: 1 85858 138 9

Typeset in Plantin and made and printed
in Great Britain by Warwick Printing Company Limited,
Caswell Road, Leamington Spa CV31 1QD

CONTENTS

FOREWORD

by Councillor Dennis Minnis
Chair of Housing Services Committee, Birmingham City Council

Carl Chinn's book is a fascinating and well-researched record of equal value to social historians and the public alike. Students of the development of social housing in the City will find much that will support their research. Those just taking a nostalgic browse through the pages will not be disappointed. Like me, many readers will have memories of a large number of locations in the fascinating photographs.

In the race to complete the five central redevelopment areas in the 50's and 60's, often poor but usually well established communities were broken up and spread right across the city – some people were put over 100 feet up in the air! These communities had taken generations to evolve and the stress put great strain on many individuals, particularly the elderly.

Some years ago I was sitting on an Inner Circle 'bus in Monument Road and overheard an elderly lady telling a friend she hadn't seen for years that she had moved under clearance to Acocks Green. This lady told her friend that she travelled from Acocks Green to Spring Hill nearly every day of the week to do her shopping, so great was the pull of what she called "the old end". Such was the wrench of being torn from your home of 50 or 60 years.

A lot still needs to be done in Birmingham and we are already beginning to demolish estates built only 30 years ago. The lessons are there for us to learn. It is essential we take heed if future communities are to take root and flourish in the way that didn't happen after our last major redevelopment.

AUTHOR'S NOTE

This book is the result of the merging of *Homes for People: 100 years of Council Housing in Birmingham* (1991) and *Keeping the City Alive: Twenty-One Years of Urban Renewal in Birmingham, 1972-93* (1993). In the light of my own research, there has been much rewriting, the inclusion of new sections and the addition of a fresh chapter to take the story through the 1990s. This enlargement has meant the inclusion of a significant number of additional photographs, all of which are credited to Birmingham City Council Housing Department unless indicated otherwise. Similarly, all memories are taken from letters written to me and deposited in my archive in Central Library. There is also a chapter arising out of a community project funded by a Quest Millennium Award to Joyce Farley, President of Community Forum. In respect of this project I appreciate the support of Joyce Farley and Val Priestman of Community Forum; of Simon Buxton and Vanessa Cusack of Quest Millennium Awards; and of Pat Robinson and Hilary Stacey of Catalyst Mediation who did ice-breaking sessions with the youngsters from the two schools involved in the project. From Kingsland Primary School, Kingstanding and Oldknow Junior School, Small Heath, the school children interviewed elderly council tenants and owner occupiers who have been affected by Urban Renewal. Finally, I thank a number of people from the Housing Department and the former Urban Renewal for their input into what is substantially a new work: Howard Pidd, Press and External Relations Manager for his backing, thoughtfulness and dedication; Pat Muddiman, Development Officer for her interest, initiative and creativity; John Downie, Urban Renewal Officer for his encouragement and advice on Chapter 4; Tony Roberts, Section Head, Development and Joint Ventures, for his constructive comments on Chapter 5; Julie Hammonds, Public Relations Manager, for her support; and all the ladies who assisted with the typing of the original books onto a disk so that I could rewrite the work more easily. Collectively known as the Word Processing Department at the Housing Department they are: Marie Nolan-Smith; Sue Ross; Lynne Stansbie; Claudette McCalla; Patricia Taylor; Pamela Barry; Barbara Prentice; Jean Scougall; Velma Dutton; Elaine Tennant; and Marilyn Kelly. My appreciation also goes to Denise Pidd for the arduous but important task of transcribing the oral history interviews. Above all, I thank my wife, Kay, for her understanding.

I dedicate this book to the memory of Our Nan, Lil Perry, and Our Aunt, Winnie Martin. Like many Brummies, these sisters were moved from back-to-backs into council maisonettes and flats. I hope I have done credit to them and to all those Brummies who endured bad housing but still strove for cleanliness and always battled to build a better world for us their children and grandchildren.

Chapter 1:

The Housing Problem, 1849-1914

Traditionalists looked on aghast as the face of Britain was altered radically in the early 1800s. With the transformation of Britain into the world's first urban, industrial society, sleepy villages and ancient market towns were overwhelmed by the explosive growth of vibrant manufacturing centres like Birmingham. Young people were drawn powerfully to the new world, their fear of the unknown beaten down by their pursuit of excitement, their search for work, their hope for a future and their expectancy of freedom. Everywhere it seemed as if the features of change, movement, youth and newness were in the ascendancy. Linked inextricably to them was a new social system. Untrammelled apparently by respect for paternalism and deference, it was based on class loyalties and it seemed to threaten the established order. No longer were factory owners content to allow the gentry to order their estate and no longer were workers willing to wait at the rich man's gate. Both groups pursued a better life; both were creating wealth; and both demanded that their voice be heard. With the rise of class antagonism and conflict, the members of the manufacturing middle class had as their bastions the great industrial towns of the Midlands and North of England. Here they proclaimed both their independence and assertiveness in their newspapers, voting patterns, lifestyle and civic buildings. As with Birmingham's Town Hall, such structures were erected in the style of Classical Greece and Rome so as to announce a bond with civilisation, culture and thought.

Looking down Congreve Street from Great Charles Street towards Victoria Square, 1873. This painting by J. Laurence Hart shows the back of the Town Hall on the right and the spire of Christchurch in the background. Soon after, the old buildings on the left were to be knocked down for the building of the Council House and the Art Gallery. (City of Birmingham Art Gallery).

Giving ground to the surge of power of the manufacturing middle class, the landed elite of Britain became converted to the politics of laissez-faire. Government ministers took pride in letting things be in social and economic matters. This non-interference had serious repercussions upon the lives of the members of the working class who made up the great majority in industrial towns. Despite the explosion in the populations of such places, little action was taken to regulate either their growth or the type of new houses which were constructed. Unhindered by planning orders, building laws and legal controls, jerry builders erected hundreds of thousands of low quality, insanitary and life-threatening houses cheek by jowl with factories and works throwing out foulness. As Friedrich Engels recounted evocatively in *The Condition of the Working Class in England* (1845), in Manchester and Salford in particular the result was appalling. Large areas had become slums – places of squalid and overcrowded housing overhung by a foul atmosphere and provided with few, if any, facilities. Unwilling to live close to these slums and wishing to escape pollution, the middle class had fled the twin towns and sought residence in spots which were cleaner, healthier and closer to the farmlands of Cheshire in the south. This stark residential segregation was as obvious elsewhere, Birmingham included. In the fifty years from 1821 its population expanded enormously from 106,000 to 343,000, and at the same time its central business district became ringed by a collar of slums dominated by back-to-backs.

These old houses are at the back of the shops and other buildings shown in J. Laurence Hart's painting on the previous page. Taken in the early 1870s, it makes clear the demolitions needed for the erection of the Council House (1874-9) and Art Gallery. Despite the destruction and dilapidation notice the line of clean washing by the woman and child in front of the two houses at the bottom. Near them, chickens are running around. The Town Hall is on the right with Christchurch on the left. (Birmingham Library Services).

Built in terraces two or three storeys high, most back-to-backs had two small bedrooms, a room downstairs, a scullery and a cellar. Normally up an entry and away from the street front, they were typically grouped six or more to a courtyard and were separated from their neighbours by merely a single brick wall. Often, dirt and not sand was used in their construction and they were infested with bugs and cockroaches, despite the cleanliness of many families. The problems of the houses themselves were exacerbated by external conditions, as was made plain by Robert Rawlinson, an inspector appointed to enquire into the public health of Birmingham in 1849. He reported that in many yards the water was drawn from wells which were 'impregnated with offensive matter' flowing in from uncleansed streets, overfull cesspits, sodden miskins (rubbish heaps) and crammed graveyards. Most of these yards were closed in on all sides, with the communal privies and cesspools crowded against them, 'and there is a distinct lack of light and ventilation'. Moreover, there were about 336 butchers in the town, most of whom had private slaughter-houses hard and fast to 'cottages'. Pig sties and heaps of manure added to the stench and the assault on health – yet even so women valiantly strove to clean the few clothes of a family in tumble-down brew'uses (wash-houses). With the River Rea, the Hockley Brook and the canals having become open sewers, contamination was everywhere. Insanitary and unhealthy, Birmingham's courtyards bred disease and quickened death.

This sketch emphasises the determination of poorer women to keep clean in defiance of the dire conditions in which they lived. The yard is sodden and the privies are probably behind the palings on the right. This yard in John Street disappeared with the cutting of Corporation Street. (The Graphic, an illustrated newspaper, 1876).

The corner of Greens Village and John Bright Street, about 1880. Greens Village was decried as a rookery, a dangerous slum area filed with criminals and roughs. In reality it was a poorer neighbourhood marked by strong kinship loyalties amongst its largely Irish inhabitants, nearly all of whom came from west of the Shannon and many of whom were from one county, Roscommon. Greens Village was cleared for the cutting of John Bright Street.

Bad housing, inadequate sanitation, and unhealthiness were not unique to Birmingham. The poor everywhere lived in life-destroying districts. Writing in 1847, Hector Gavin explained that in Surrey 'the mean duration of life' was forty-five years, in London it was thirty seven, and in Liverpool it was just twenty six. And although the poor were most badly affected by insanitary conditions, still a middle-class Londoner or Liverpudlian could expect to live less than his or her counterpart in Surrey. The general danger of town living was stressed by the terrible cholera epidemic of 1848. Fearful of the spread of disease and with a Christian conscience pricked by the dreadful living conditions suffered by the poor, the upper and middles classes listened to the arguments put forward by reformers and supported the passing of the Public Health Act (1848). Unfortunately, the legislation was mostly permissive and local authorities only adopted its provisions if they so wished. Some did so strenuously, and a few vigorously sought other powers to improve life in their towns. In particular, Liverpool was a progressive corporation. In 1846 it had passed a Sanitary Act peculiar to the city and a year later it appointed the country's first medical officer of health. These actions were followed by serious attempts to improve the supplies of gas and water. Manchester, too, tried to make an impact on slum conditions by banning the building of back-to-backs from 1844. By contrast, Birmingham was markedly sluggish in its response to the problems posed by unplanned urban growth.

First elected in 1838, Birmingham's council did not become responsible for sewerage, drainage and the regulation of sanitary conditions until 1851. Even then councillors did not distinguish themselves by their commitment to public health reform. Dominated by 'the economists', those who wished to spend little and keep the rates down, the corporation became notorious for its inactivity and parsimony. Next to nothing was done to improve the living conditions of the town's poor. Indeed, their problems became worse as the improvements of private developers led to the consolidation of Birmingham's central shopping and business area. One of the town's first major slum clearances came when mean streets such as Peck Lane, The Froggery and Old Meeting Street disappeared with the building of New Street Station (1846-53). This was followed in the 1860s and 1870s by the demolition of squalid property on the Colmore Estate, leading to the emergence of new rows of imposing buildings around Edmund Street and Newhall Street. This destruction by the developers improved the appearance of the city and rid it of unhealthy slums, but the motivation was profit and not concern for the plight of the poor. Neither the developers nor councillors gave any thought to rehousing those made homeless by their schemes. Needing to live in the cheapest accommodation close to the markets where they bought their bits of food and near to the sources of irregular employment, the displaced poor pushed themselves tightly into adjoining slums in the central wards of the city.

The demolition of old property on the Colmore Estate, from which emerged Birmingham's financial centre. Notice the railings of St Philip's Cathedral on the right. Just beyond the lamp-post on the left is Church Street, on the corner of which the Grand Hotel would be opened in 1879.

By the late 1860s, the economists were faced with strong opposition. Inspired by preachers like George Dawson at the Church of the Saviour and Robert Dale at Carrs Lane Church, influential men proclaimed the Civic Gospel that the wealthy had a duty to improve life for all the citizens of Birmingham. Although they were capitalists and Liberals, they realised that some interference by the council was necessary for the welfare of the community and they proposed that public services vital for good health ought to be owned by the local authority. Under the mayoralty of Joseph Chamberlain (1873-1876) the supporters of this municipal socialism controlled the corporation and implemented far-reaching measures: the council took control of the town's gas and water companies; a bye-law effectively forbade the building of back-to-backs; landlords were forced to close polluted wells and connect their properties with the town water supply, usually via a standpipe in each yard; the sewerage farm at Saltley was improved and extended; a drainage board was established; and unhealthy open middens began to be replaced by lavatories with a metal pan under each seat. These were emptied weekly by the council, as were the wooden tubs put in each yard for the collection of dry ashes and rubbish. From 1872, the town's health was monitored by Dr Hill, its first medical officer, who reported to a Health Committee after 1875, and sanitary inspectors were appointed to deal with 'nuisances', ranging from adulterated food and infectious diseases to filthy courts. No longer were the horrendous problems of slum life to be ignored.

Houses in Thomas Street which were to be knocked down for the cutting of Corporation Street, about 1882. (Birmingham Library Services). Like Old Square and John Street, it had been laid out in the early 1700s by John Pemberton, a wealthy ironmaster and financier. As with Greens Village, both John and Thomas Streets were denigrated as rookeries. Photographs such as this strip away the bad reputations of the folk who lived here and give them back their humanity.

Ill health and bad housing were the twin evils which bedevilled and blighted the lives of the city's poor. The link between the two was inextricable, as was made graphic by Birmingham's Medical Officer of Health in 1875. He drew attention to the difference between the annual death rate in wealthy Edgbaston at 13.11 per thousand with that of the poor St Mary's Ward (the Gun Quarter) at 26.82. Between ten and twelve thousand people lived in the ward and their dreadful environment was called forth by William White, a well-respected Quaker and Liberal Councillor. Many of the dwellings were dilapidated, their floors were damp, and they suffered through the oozing of filth through the walls, 'causing horrible stenches'. Unsurprisingly, sickness was rife. Such a situation demanded drastic action. Under the Artisans' Dwellings Act of 1875, corporations were given power to acquire, demolish and redevelop slum areas. Birmingham Council used this law to make the ward the subject of an improvement scheme. Property was compulsory purchased and cleared, and a wide road was formed. Aptly called Corporation Street, by 1889 the bottom section from Bull Street to New Street was filled with fine new buildings. This Parisian-style boulevard reflected Birmingham's dignity and position as the metropolis of the Midlands, yet as the prestigious new street advanced, the poor of St Mary's Ward were shunned. A slum was erased, but no thought was given to the needs of those who had lost their homes.

Looking up from Stephenson Place towards the bottom end of Corporation Street, early 1890s. The statue is that of Thomas Attwood, the leader of the Birmingham Political Union and a major figure in the movement which pushed for the Great Reform Act of 1832. It is now in Sparkbrook, close to the site of one his houses, 'The Larches'. The stretch of Corporation Street between New Street and Bull Street was the most prestigious for retailers. Its emergence had entailed the demolition of much property that was not regarded as slum, a move which reinforced beliefs that the new thoroughfare was less about improving conditions for the poor and more about creating a shopping road to enhance Birmingham's prestige.

In pushing forward the Improvement Scheme, Chamberlain had stressed two objectives: the need to improve conditions for the working class; and the desire to enhance the look and reputation of Birmingham. As the project went forward, it became apparent that the latter aim was uppermost in the minds of the Improvement Committee. Overseeing the removal of slum buildings and the construction of Corporation Street, it could have sought permission from the government to build working-class housing on some of the cleared sites. It did not do so. Slowly condemnation grew at the lack of concern shown by the council for the poor who had been ejected from their homes without any choice or any say. In 1885 the committee was prompted to action by the charge that only middle-class residents had benefited from the improvement. A plan was prepared for the erection of flats for working-class people in Dalton Street. Despite some vigorous support, the council rejected it, believing that private developers would build houses to replace those cleared. By 1889 the disinterest of the private sector was glaring, so the committee proposed building twenty-two houses in Ryder Street, on a site left vacant for development since 1883. The scheme was small-scale considering that 855 dwellings had been demolished by the improvement scheme and 5,000 people had been 'unhoused', and it did nothing to solve the housing problems of the poor. Still, it encountered considerable opposition before it was passed. Built at a cost of £182 each, the houses were finished in September 1890 and were rented out a 5s 6d (27½p) a week.

Mrs Annie Storey and her daughter, Maisie, tenants of Birmingham's first council houses in the yard at the back of 63, Ryder Street, 1949/50. (Mrs Maisie Harrison and Jim Storey).

Mrs Margaret Roberts aged 100.

Frederick Lewis, the owner of a demolition firm, helping to knock down D terrace of the council houses in Lawrence Street, 15 January 1972. This was the last remaining block of the four which had stood locally and despite a determined campaign to preserve them, they were cleared as part of the expansion plans for Aston University. (Birmingham Evening Mail). Now 100 years old, Margaret Roberts (nee Willey) was born in Nova Scotia Street off Corporation Street, but as a child her family moved to Lawrence Street 'into one of the very first council houses that Birmingham built. It was wonderful for us. We was the third one in.' There were eight houses each side of a court, with a lamp in the middle, and upstairs each had a great big attic. Margaret's two brothers slept there and 'it was like a gym up there' with everything they had for boxing: 'And do you know there was only us that hasn't got a policeman living in the house. They was either lodgers, or sons or husbands. They was all in the police force. And at the bottom of Lawrence Street was a police station.' (Margaret Roberts, Carl Chinn Show, BBC WM, May, 9 1999).

The Ryder Street houses were let quickly, encouraging the committee in 1891 to counter criticism by making a more extensive proposal for nearby Lawrence Street. Costing £172 each, eighty-two similar houses were built, rented at between 5s and 7s 6d a week. Despite the objections of those opposed to public involvement in housing, the council had shown that it was able to compete successfully with private enterprise. It had built good quality houses, let at moderate rents, and without serious loss to the ratepayers. Still, it had not addressed the difficulty of slum housing. Firstly, the project was too limited. Secondly, the houses were let to families of a 'good class' – only 'respectable' well-paid working-class people were wanted as tenants, not the poor. And thirdly, even the lowest rental of 5s (25p) a week was too much for a poor family which might only be bringing in 17s 6d (87$\frac{1}{2}$p) a week. Yet Liberals continued to believe in containing the slums by a cautious policy of forcing repairs upon property owners until private enterprise solved the housing problem. This was to be achieved by the movement of skilled working-class people into new houses so that their former homes could be taken over by the poor. Such an approach ignored the reality that in 1884 there were 27,000 houses in Birmingham let at 3s 6d (17$\frac{1}{2}$p) a week or less. The majority were insanitary and defective. In support of their stance Liberals stressed the unfeasibility of wholesale slum clearance because of the huge cost in building replacement houses cheap enough to rent by the poor.

The continuing plight of the poor was emphasised in 1893 when Dr Alfred Hill inspected the sanitary condition of two poor areas, Woodcock Street and Milk Street. His report could have applied to most neighbourhoods in the central parts of the city. None of the property was good. The houses were back-to-back, with deteriorated roofs, floors, sinks, walls and wash-houses. They were damp, having leaky roofs and porous quarries as floors, and they were without damp-courses; whilst the yards were unpaved and sodden with filth. The buildings of the districts were badly arranged, so that they crowded closely together, and some were very obstructive: for example, the first house in number one court Milk Street was only seven feet from other dwellings. Dr Hill concluded that the construction of the houses in both localities led to a lack of light and fresh air. Together with the damp and generally bad drainage and sewerage, this caused a danger to the health of the poor who lived there. Two years later he provided tragic statistical evidence for this conclusion. After taking a population census for the Milk Street area, he estimated that its death rate was twice as high as the average for the city. He recommended that the only remedy for the district was to make it subject to an improvement scheme which would re-arrange and re-construct its streets and houses.

The two women sitting with their backs to the front of the house are chopping firewood in a courtyard in Digbeth, about 1908. They are wearing hurden gowns, made from the thick hessian used for hard-wearing sacks. Notice at how the yard is overshadowed by the railway viaduct. The two women in the doorway and the woman on the rocking chair look as if they might be helpers from the Digbeth Institute, set up by members of Carrs Lane Church as a place where poorer folk could find help and entertainment.

Young lads playing marlies in the gutter outside the flats in Rea Terrace, Milk Street – across the railway lines from Digbeth and close to the junction with Bordesley Street and Little Anne Street, probably late 1940s. (Geoff Dowling).

The Housing of the Working Classes Act of 1890 allowed the council to prepare improvement schemes outside the Corporation Street area. Consequently, in 1894 Dr Hill's recommendation was accepted by the Improvement Committee. It was proposed to compulsory purchase the buildings in those parts of the Woodcock Street and Milk Street areas which were declared as insanitary, to demolish them and build 116 houses upon the sites. Because of the cost involved in buying the scheduled buildings, there was determined opposition to this plan within the council. As a compromise, the unhealthy houses in Woodcock Street were dropped from the scheme. In 1895 Parliament approved the proposals for Milk Street. Within two years, half of the site of sixty-five dwellings and a few workshops was cleared for building and the remainder was unoccupied. Plans were drawn up to replace them with 64 dual-system houses, each of three rooms. Those dwellings on the lower tier would have rents of 4s 3d (21½p) per week and those on the upper tier rents of 3s 9d (19p) a week. The committee was satisfied that this was the only way to build homes in the central area of the city, at a rental low enough for labourers and without a loss to the rate-payers. A majority of councillors objected vehemently to the plan and it was withdrawn. Finally, in 1898 it was agreed to construct four two-storey blocks of tenements. The sixty-one homes of between two and four rooms were finished in 1900 and let at between 3s (15p) and 5s (25p) a week.

During the 1870s and 1880s, Birmingham had appeared intent upon transforming the living conditions of its poor. The council and private enterprise had destroyed some of the city's worst slums, whilst the corporation had also implemented a number of reforms crucial for better health. These improvements had led to a marked fall in the city's mortality rate, from 25.2 deaths for every thousand people between 1871-75 to 20.7 by 1881-85. According to the respected historian Asa Briggs, 'the averages for the whole city, always misleading, do not express the full measure of benefit reaped by the "black-spot" districts'. There can be little doubt that under the impetus of Joseph Chamberlain there had been progress, so much so that in 1881 the corporation declared that with regards to health the town was now first amongst all the large urban centres of Great Britain. Its satisfaction was bolstered by the comments of J. Ralph, an American writer, who exclaimed in 1890 that Birmingham was 'the best-governed city in the world'. In reality, the task of improvement was only half-done. The council had set its face resolutely against massive slum clearance and the building of corporation houses on a large scale. This policy, allied with continued piecemeal demolitions, led to deteriorating conditions in the poorer parts of Birmingham. Apart from a few concerned churchmen and councillors, there seemed little interest in the misery of the poor. Indeed, many better-off people presumed that slums had disappeared from enlightened Birmingham and were but a memory. Soon they were to be shocked out of their apathy.

Some of the folk of Number 1 Court, Thomas Street, about 1882. These people would soon be faced with having to find new homes following the demolition of this property for the cutting of Corporation Street. The youngster in the foreground has a patch covering his right eye, whilst five of the six men are wearing billycocks – bowlers hats. This was the working-class headgear until the coming of the flat cap later in the century. (Birmingham Library Services).

During the 1880s, Britain was shaken out of its complacency as the wealthiest and most powerful nation in the world by publications highlighting the persistence of poverty amidst plenty. This 'rediscovery of poverty' made little impact upon Birmingham until 1898 when the Reverend T.J. Bass sought to arouse public opinion by recounting the dire poverty in the parish of St Laurence, Gosta Green. His book, *Every Day in Blackest Birmingham. Facts not Fiction*, appealed for God 'to awaken those within this parish and those outside it, to a sense of duty, so that such neighbourhoods may no longer be left in their darkness but may be illuminated by the "Light of Light"'. It was followed in 1899 by a pamphlet on *The Housing of the Poor* by John Arthur Fellows. He and other socialists advocated the sweeping away of the slums in the central wards and the development of low-density council house estates on the edge of the city. The growing debate over housing reform was strengthened by an investigation by Dr Alfred Hill into the city's 43,366 back-to-backs grouped in about 6,000 courts. Also published in 1899, it revealed that most such dwellings were rented at 3s 6d or less a week. In St Bartholomew's Ward (east of Digbeth), over 50% of the houses were in this category and the annual death was 32.7 per thousand people. In areas with no such houses, the death rate was dramatically lower at 17.1. Each year because of insanitary, badly-built, back-to-back houses, 3,000 people died who would have lived given better housing. More horrific was the infant mortality rate. The conclusion was inescapable. Poverty murdered. The birth right of the poor was a high death rate; their inheritance the dreadful conditions in which they struggled to live.

Two-storey back-to-backs at 4-7, Lincoln Place, Garrison Lane, Bordesley, about 1905. This was just up from Gray Street. Despite the wretched condition of the houses the woman in the doorway is making a valiant effort to show her respectability with crocheted net covering the downstairs window of her home. This photograph is from the 'Slum Collection'. As part of Nettlefold's push to improve the worst property, photographs were taken before work was carried out and sometimes whilst it was going on and after it was finished. The collection is a moving one, stressing the hardships faced by poorer Brummies but making clear their pride and cleanliness. (Birmingham Library Services).

Despite the pleas of Bass and Fellows, it seemed as if the bitter cry of the poor went unheard in Birmingham. The council itself exemplified the general indifference. Riven between Liberals, Conservatives and Liberal Unionists – those who had followed Chamberlain in his break with the Liberals in the 1880s – it did not seem to have the corporate will to act decisively. However, in 1901 it was driven into movement by the publication of a series of explicit articles in the Conservative supporting *Birmingham Daily Gazette*. Written by J. Cuming Walters and motivated as much by political considerations as by social concern, they were called *Scenes in Slumland* and they made a number of shocking revelations. He exclaimed that the pen of a Zola could scarcely do justice to the filthy horrors in some of the slums of Birmingham, 'in Christian England, and in the best-governed city in the world, with the finest Health Committee and the most enterprising municipality ever known'. Five aldermen and the Deputy Chairman of the Health Committee were denounced as owners of slum property. A furore was caused and Cuming Walters was sued for libel, but the indignation of the citizens of Birmingham was woken and there was sustained agitation demanding that something be done about the housing question. In June 1901 this led to a bad-tempered debate in the council which focused on a power struggle between Alderman Cook, the Liberal chairman of the Health Committee, and an aspiring, younger Liberal Unionist councillor, J. S. Nettlefold. Supported by the Conservatives, Nettlefold won and by 32 votes to 30 the council agreed to set up a new Housing Committee.

Numbers 1 and 2, number 2 Court, Tower Street, Summer Lane neighbourhood, about 1905. This is a very poignant photograph with the child huddled in the entry and the other leaning against the wall. ('Slum Collection', Birmingham Library Services).

Children in the Ideal Park at Little Bromwich, early 1900s. The park lies between Marchmont Road, Daniels Road, Bordesley Green and Finnemore Road. Even at a distance, the superiority of the houses on the estate compared to those in central Birmingham are obvious. They are more modern, larger, clearly better constructed and set in a better environment.

Chairman of the Health Committee since 1874, Cook defended himself strongly against his critics. He pointed out that since 1891, the corporation had demolished 536 dwellings and more had been shut down by property owners unable or unwilling to make the sanitary improvements demanded of them. Without replacement dwellings, the result was increased overcrowding and higher rents for slum dwellings. In these circumstances, widescale slum clearance could be a dehousing policy. Indeed, in response to the glaring need for new dwellings, Cook and his Health Committee had shifted towards the opinion that a large housing scheme was needed on the outskirts of the city. To this end, in 1900 it brought seventeen acres of land at Bordesley Green, planning to build upon it 621 houses to be rented at between 3s 9d (19p) and 5s (25p) a week. Additionally, for those working-class folk who could not afford the move to the suburbs, it was proposed that two, four-storey blocks of tenements be erected on a plot in Potter Street. This response was resisted fiercely by councillors from across the political spectrum who opposed municipal house-building and believed that the solution to the slum problem was to be found in private enterprise. In particular, Liberal Unionists were against any subsidies to council house building via the rates. Cook's proposal were rejected. The Potter Street Scheme passed in to oblivion, and in 1908 the site at Bordesley Green was leased to the Ideal Benefit Society to develop houses for working-class ownership in a garden-city environment. Birmingham's housing problem remained seemingly intractable.

The new Housing Committee took over all powers exercised under the housing acts and such powers under the public health acts as was thought desirable. Chaired by the energetic J. S. Nettlefold, it set out its intentions out firmly in 1902 when the Reverend Bass and others requested that an improvement scheme be brought in for the Oxygen Street neighbourhood of Duddeston. Under Part 1 of the Housing of the Working Classes Act 1890, the clearance of an insanitary area would have required the rehousing of those who lost their homes. However, Part 2 of the law enabled the corporation to deal with insanitary dwellings singly and without rehousing or the payment of compensation to the owners. The Housing Committee preserved this approach. Of course, most owners of dilapidated property were keen to avoid demolition and remedied sanitary and drainage defects by putting in damp courses, opening windows, and repairing roofs, floors and walls. Derided by Radical Conservatives and Labour supporters as 'slum patching', the policy of property improvement was accompanied elsewhere in central Birmingham by the limited demolition of slum dwellings for one of two reasons. Firstly, where repairs were not carried out; and secondly, to open up a courtyard to light and air by knocking down the house on either side of its entry. Such yards became known as 'Nettlefold Courts'. Between 1901 and 1906, 1,132 houses were made fit to live in, 522 were demolished and 41 courts were opened to the street. It was admitted that this policy was not drastic, but it remained unchanged until 1914.

Improvement of two-storey back-to-backs at Number 11 Court, rear of 80, Aston Road, half way between Mill Street and Dartmouth Street about 1908. Notice the addition of bay windows, the fitting of new doors and roofs, and the laying of proper drainage facilities. ('Slum Collection', Birmingham Library Services).

In Birmingham's poorer neighbourhoods the housing stock was ageing and deteriorating. Faced with mounting structural and sanitary problems, the policy of slum patching could be no more than a short-term measure. However, it was the only way in which the lives of poor people could be improved until enough councillors recognised the need for a substantial investment by the corporation in slum clearance and council house building. Together with better health care, the approach did lead to a fall in both infant mortality and general death rates in the city's poverty stricken central wards. This improvement should be acknowledged but not exaggerated. The poor remained more likely to die than the better off, just because they were poor and lived in slum housing. This was shown graphically by an investigation in 1909 and 1910 into the wards of St Stephen's and St George's (parts of Hockley, Summer Lane and Newtown Row). It divided the population according to the weekly income of the head of the household. In that group where the wage was 20s a week or more, the infant mortality rate was 140; in the group where the income was less than 20s a week, this rose distressingly to 210. Furthermore, the babies of the poorer section who survived to the age of twelve months were, on average, 1lb less in weight than the babies born to more prosperous parents. Clearly, life expectancy and health were impaired by a low income and the rent of an insanitary house.

A Nettlefold Court at Number 2, William Street, close to the junction with St Martin's Street, about 1909. William Street runs between Granville Street and Islington Row in the Bath Row neighbourhood. The houses have been improved and the yard has been opened up by the demolition of property which had blocked it off from the street. Look at the spotless white pinners on the baby and young girl at the yard's entrance. ('Slum Collection', Birmingham Library Service).

Young children playing with a chair close to the communal lavatories, about 1920. The lavatory in the middle is a water closet, those on either side are dry pan privies – wooden seats with a large round hole and in a square box and a receptacle beneath them. In her book, Her People, *(1982) Kathleen Dayus told how 'us children had to hold the sides of the seat otherwise we could have fallen in. These were dry closets. You can imagine the stench in the summer.' On the house wall behind the lavatories is a memorial to local men who died in The First World War. I showed this photo at Small Heath Local History Society and several people were certain that it is Arthur Street, where there was such a memorial. (Birmingham Library Services).*

By the late 1890s, Alderman Cook had recognised that Birmingham's approach to municipal house building 'did not touch the fringe of the question' on how to provide good and affordable housing for the poor. His comments were as applicable to the years during which the Housing Committee was in control and despite improvements to slum property, sanitation in the courtyards of Birmingham remained appalling. Allegedly 'competent witnesses' felt that a common tap in the courtyard and a neighbouring gully were sufficient to provide water for all its residents and to drain away the slop water. Dr Robertson, Birmingham's Medical Officer of Health from 1903, disagreed. He argued that if poor people were to win their battle for cleanliness then each house needed its own sink and water supply as a minimal requirement. Yet common taps remained widespread, and a few vile, unhealthy midden privies remained. Irregularly cleaned, human refuse overspilled from them into courtyards and houses. From the 1870s most were replaced by dry privies with a pan below the seat. Supposedly emptied once a week, they were shared by several families and were inadequate, smelly, unhealthy, and lacking in privacy. With such deficient facilities it was not surprising that disease was rife in poorer neighbourhoods and that diarrhoea slaughtered many children unnecessarily. Healthier water closets were universal in middle-class houses, but they were not introduced in to courtyards because the city's Water Department had an insufficient supply of water. This class-biased reason disappeared upon completion of the Elan Valley works in 1904, and water closets began to replace dry pan privies in the slums.

Fu or outsiders, a slum was not just bad housing but a way of life. 'Slummie' became a derogatory term evoking a picture of dirty, rough and unpleasant people. In reality, there was more heroism in poorer neighbourhoods than ever can be assessed. Tens of thousands of people fought to survive with dignity a life of low pay, ill-health, under-nourishment and inadequate housing. Too often, observers from another class were oblivious to their continuous battle against a hostile environment. Those who employed poor women to do their washing and cleaning could never comprehend the hard work involved in staying clean. Dirty clothes had to be maided with a dolly in a tub and then scrubbed in a smaller one – arduous tasks in themselves. After these tasks, the clothes were boiled in the copper in the brew 'us. This held about twenty gallons of water, filled by the bucketful from the tap in the yard – whatever the weather. Next washing was swilled in a tub of water and Reckitt's Blue, then starched. This operation was followed by mangling, hanging out and ironing. Finally, water from the copper was used to scrub wooden toilet seats, stairs and floorboards. Other heavy cleaning tasks for wives included black-leading the grate, polishing brasses, whitening the hearth, and red ochreing the front step. Surrounded by factories belching out smoke and dirt, the wonder is that so many women won their never-ending battle against dirt.

Women washing in the brew'us in the yard at the back of 131, Fazeley Street, between Pickford Street and Barn Street, Digbeth about 1905. The women are carrying out their tasks even though the wash house has no glass in the window. Above them is shopping – the term used to describe small workshops at the back of housing. In his unpublished autobiography, In Victoria's Image, *my great-uncle Wal Chinn wrote that 'not all had despaired of change, with many making every effort to be clean and pleasant in appearance, to do them credit with no modern aids available, just soap and water plus elbow grease.'*

Since the 1860s, speculative builders had erected houses in outlying districts for the better-paid of the working class. By the 1880s, areas like Sparkbrook, Saltley and Winson Green were mostly covered with six-roomed tunnel-back dwellings, each with its own back garden and lavatory but no bathroom. Migration was encouraged by the building of suburban factories and by bicycles, trams and railways which enabled workers to live further than walking distance from their jobs. Increasingly, the central wards of Birmingham were left to the poor. Before 1914 the poverty line was acknowledged to be an income of 18s-21s (90p – £1.05p) a week. Unskilled workers in regular jobs were unlikely to earn this, and for most labourers employment was irregular. Daily they searched for the casual work more likely to be found in the workshops, factories and street trading of the central areas than in the suburbs. As a woman explained to the journalist Cuming Walters, 'Why don't I leave? Because I can't get a house any better near my husband's work, or near the school the children go to. We've got no choice. We're obliged to take the houses we can afford.' The unskilled were caught in an unenviable position. Too poor to move, they were having to pay the increased rents caused by the council's housing policy of limited demolition and improvement of dwellings. In 1905 the Health Department recorded a sample of 243 houses it had dealt with. Demolitions had reduced the number to 226, whilst average rents had risen from 3s 8d (18p) a week to 4s 3d (21$\frac{1}{2}$p). Consequently, tenants were paying interest on half the cost of the landlord's repairs on their properties. The straitjacket of poverty was pulled tighter.

Garden in a yard in Sherbourne Road near to Longmore Street, Balsall Heath, about 1910. Mrs Gilbert sits beside her daughter, Ethel, whilst another daughter, Elizabeth, stands behind her brother Edwin (Ted). Despite the unfavourable conditions, many poorer folk cultivated lovely gardens. (Mr A. G. Tinley, son of Ethel).

In 1904, a report on the 10,000 people of the Floodgate Street area revealed a death rate 60% higher than the city's average; and in Park Street it was a grim 63 per 1,000 people compared to 12.1 in Edgbaston. Not surprisingly, two thirds of houses in the street were back-to-backs and most of the men were unskilled labourers and street traders earning between 17s (85p) and 21s (£1.05p) a week. The conclusion was unequivocal. Wages in the central wards made it impossible for a labourer to keep a wife and family out of poverty. To earn enough just for rent, clothing and fuel, it was essential that wives and children worked. The jobs open to them were ill-paid, tiring and repetitive: wrapping up hair pins in paper – ten to the paper with one outside to hold the pack together – at 2d a 1,000; carding safety pins at 2d (less than 1p) a gross (144) if there were nine pins of different sizes on each card; and varnishing pen-holders at 1d (less than $^1\!/_2$p) a gross. Other laborious tasks involved selling firewood, carding of hooks and eyes, and the sewing of buttons on to cards. According to Robert Sherard in *The Child Slaves of Britain (1905)*, the wages for such work could only be calculated in 'infinitesimal fractions of pence'. Mothers and children had to take sweated jobs to stave off starvation and stay out of the hated workhouse. They had to live in decrepit back-to-backs close to their work, which was found in the central wards not the healthier suburbs.

Women outside the Floodgate Street Infant Welfare Centre, about 1910. This was set up by a number of concerned middle-class women, amongst them Mrs Caswell. She was a teacher of the Women's Adult School and was impelled to act after one day she had visited a poor woman in Deritend. On leaving she noticed a very poor looking young woman 'sitting at an old table with a glue pot and making paper boxes. At her side was an old Pram with a tin of condensed milk beside. the young mother was dipping a teat in it, putting it into the child's mouth to stop it from crying. It was a hot day. The Courtyard smelled awful. . . down the child's front where the milk dribbled was covered with Blow flies, it turned me sick.' Mrs Caswell spoke to the husband who was smoking inside the house. He berated her to mind her own business and added that he needed his wife's money for a bet. Mrs Caswell got in touch with the Health Department and the mother and child were taken to hospital where sadly they died. On the right of the photograph, wearing the black hat and holding the baby in the shawl, is Sarah Webster of Bolton Road, Small Heath. I put this shot in the Evening Mail *and Sarah was recognised by Ivy Matthews who later married Frank Webster. (*Sparkhill and Greet Maternity and Infant Welfare Centre, *unpublished, 1920, thanks to Ivy Caswell).*

Escape from the meshes of poverty was difficult. Poor people could only afford harmful housing, and that had to be near the firms which provided casual and sweated employment. In the central wards, back-to-backs vied for space with works, warehouses, shops, railway lines and canal wharves. Factories and workshops were common in courtyards, and often houses were not even separated structurally from them. This proximity damaged further the health of poor people. Industry made the atmosphere smoky, dirty, gloomy and sunless, it discharged poison, and it masked overcrowding in the deprived wards. In 1908 the number of persons per acre in St Stephen's Ward was 132.7 and in St George's it was 162.1. This compared to an average for the city of 44.2. However, works of various kinds were numerous in both districts, so that these density figures did not represent the true overcrowding of space. The real nature of the problem of overcrowding was highlighted by the atrocious situation in the Oxygen Street area. This district, which included Great Lister, Adams, Heneage and Dartmouth Streets comprised fourteen acres, of which only eight were occupied by housing. Here, 2,429 people crowded into 589 dwellings, giving a population density of 272 persons per acre of inhabited land, six times as much as the average for the city. Together with bad housing, the nearness of industry, and poverty, this abominable overcrowding in the area led to twice as many deaths each year as in Birmingham as a whole.

Children outside 102-4, Bagot Street, off Lancaster Street, about 1905. Two of the youngsters are barefooted. This photograph highlights the closeness of homes to industrial premises. In Down East Amongst the Poorest *(1905), Reverend Bass declared, 'Oxygen Street – ye gods, what a name for a street where atmosphere, polluted by neighbouring works, made my throat and nose smart and eyes run . . .' ('Slum Collection', Birmingham Library Services).*

Mother and children chopping and bundling firewood in the downstairs room of a back-to-back. The black-leaded range is behind the boy with the donkey-fringe hair cut. The poorest families did this job to try and survive. Notice there is not even a pegged rug on the floor. These were made by women who bodged rags onto hurden sacking. This is a very unusual photograph showing the inside of a poorer person's house. (Edward Cadbury, M. Cécile Matheson and George Shann, Women's Work and Wages. A Phase of Life in an Industrial City, *1906).*

The survey of the Oxygen Street area had indicated that each household numbered 4.1 people. This statistic from a desperately poor neighbourhood seemed to confirm the belief that in Birmingham the overcrowding of houses was not a problem. Such statistics were misleading, simply because they represented an average. The high birth rate in poorer districts ensured that many households greatly exceeded four in number. Large families were common, and children had to sleep top to tail in the cramped two-bedroom accommodation of back-to-backs, with fathers and older brothers often sleeping in the single room downstairs. In some homes, poverty led to the taking in of lodgers to help pay the rent and overcrowding was made worse. The problem was exacerbated by a shortage of housing in the central areas, which became obvious by 1913. Demolition of insanitary property increased after the passing of the Housing and Town Planning Act, 1909, and by 1911, in St Bartholomew's Ward alone, there were 874 houses fewer than there had been in 1896. Similar great decreases were recorded for the other central wards of St Mary's, Market Hall, St Paul's, St Thomas's, St Martin's, St Stephen's and St George's. Economic reasons ensured that most of the poor made homeless could not move to the suburbs. Consequently, the demand rose on the remaining houses in the centre. Rents went up and overcrowding increased. Unless the demolished houses were replaced quickly by cheap and decent housing, the housing problem could only become worse.

Although Birmingham's housing policy was fixed firmly, councillors were interested in other approaches to solving the housing question. In 1905 a Deputation from Nettlefold's Housing Committee visited Berlin and six other German cities. In the same year, an enquiry team which included W. J. Davis, the renowned Brummie trade-union leader, compared the lives of the city's brass workers with those of the German capital. Both groups thought that German children were better dressed, tended and well mannered, and that the lifestyle of the workers was more 'wholesome' than that of the Brummie working class. Nettlefold's group felt that the German houses they visited were cleaner and tidier, but it disliked the preponderance of flats, and found the accommodation inferior to that of Birmingham. It believed that the lighting, ventilation, and sanitary conditions of the houses were worse, and that the average room space occupied by each family was smaller. It might be wondered at how bad the German flats were if back-to-backs were considered superior to them. Yet, one important lesson was learned from the Germans – the significance of town planning. The Deputation recommended that the council should seek larger powers to control the building of new areas, aiming to ensure a better distribution of houses and the building of wide arterial roads for through traffic. Also, it advised the council to buy and lay out land in the suburbs, mark out open spaces, and encourage the building of houses at a rental available for working-class people. The proposals were approved. They signified the beginning of the Town Planning Movement in England.

Women in Court Number 7, William Street, about 1905. The attic high (three storey) back-to-backs are fronting on to the street and blocking off light and fresh air from the two storey back-to-backs in the yard. ('Slum Collection', Birmingham Library Services).

Town planning of the kind envisaged by the Housing Committee was present in the Birmingham region, but it was not directed by the council. The Cadbury brothers decided to move their chocolate works from the city to the open fields of Bournville in 1879, believing that it would be better for their work people to live in the country. In 1895, to make houses available to them, George Cadbury bought 140 acres of land near the factory and set up the Bournville Village Trust to develop it. Unlike the jerry-built, unhealthy back-to-backs of Birmingham which were erected without any thought of town planning, these new houses were well-built, spacious, sanitary and open to the air and light. They were grouped in pairs, threes, or fours and set back 20 feet from wide, tree-lined roads. There were gardens to the front, vegetable gardens at the back, and one-tenth of the estate was reserved for open spaces. Initially, 143 houses were sold on ground leases of 999 years – to prevent infilling on the gardens; and later more were built to rent. This careful town planning had astounding effects: in 1915, Bournville's infant mortality rate was 47, compared to 187 in St Mary's Ward, whilst the general death rate was eight compared to 24.5. But the poor did not share in the benefits of Bournville. It was not intended for them, rather the better-paid of the working class, those thought respectable and worthy. Fresh air, a healthy environment and decent housing still remained unattainable for the poor.

The first houses on the Bournville Estate, 232-222, Maryvale Road, 1895. Building is going on in the background and the youth of the trees indicates how recently these houses had been completed. George Cadbury's dream was 'to make it easier for working men to own houses with large gardens secure from the danger of being spoilt either by . . . factories or by interference with the enjoyment of sun, light and air'. (Philip Henslow, Ninety Years On, *1984).*

Encouraged by the German example and by Bournville, the idea of municipal town planning took hold in Birmingham. Indeed, the term itself was coined in the City in 1906 at talks in the office of Dr Robertson. Nettlefold was keen on the concept because he believed that it was an essential means whereby corporations could prevent the emergence of new slums in the suburbs. With the zeal of converts, he and Robertson began discussions with housing reformers in other towns, sending out 'missionaries' to explain the benefits of town planning. Following a conference in Manchester, the idea was taken up nationally and in 1909 a Housing and Town Planning Act was passed. This empowered municipalities to make town-planning schemes regarding land that was under development, subject to the approval of a national board. The vision of the pioneers of the town planning movement was to transform the dismal industrial towns of England into pleasant garden cities, built according to the Bournville model. Yet, to realise this dream fully, councils would have to build municipal houses and spend vast sums of money. Birmingham was not ready to do this. Most councillors now recognised that the city had to supervise – and to an extent control – the character of new development, if only to prevent the emergence of new slums. They remained to be persuaded that the most vital aspect of town planning was the building of corporation houses.

Bare-footed youngsters in a Digbeth yard, about 1910. Our Nan, Lil Perry (nee Wood), was born four years later and grew up in Whitehouse Street, Aston Cross in a back-to-back like many others with just two bedrooms. The kids 'slept four in a bed, top and bottom. Lads in the same room. 'Cus there was only Billy and Georgie lads, but as they got older they had to sleep downstairs.'

Ebrook Lane, Pype Hayes, 1893. As part of Erdington, this rural area joined Birmingham in 1911 and during the inter-war years was developed for council housing.

Edwardian Birmingham was congested. In the heavily-built up central wards there were few playgrounds and these were inadequate for large populations – as was the Park Street Gardens which served the 2,600 children of the Floodgate Street neighbourhood. Elsewhere there were neither enough parks nor the opportunity for the implementation of town planning principles which so required space. Only in Edgbaston, Harborne and East Birmingham were there wide areas of undeveloped land – and because of the middle-class nature of the two former districts it was unlikely that any working-class housing would be allowed there. The reality of too little land for town planning development was recognised by Dr Robertson. He argued that the population pressure on the over-crowded central wards could be relieved only if decent, low-rent houses were built on undeveloped sites outside the city boundary – although he did not specify by whom. Furthermore, he understood that poorer people would not move unless they could return to the city for work via a rapid and cheap transport system. His farsighted scheme gained support, but it was not practicable until 1911 when Birmingham extended its boundaries and gained swathes of farmland in Erdington, Kings Norton, Northfield, and Yardley. The importance of this extension cannot be exaggerated. With the inclusion also of Aston and Handsworth, Birmingham's size increased by 30,000 acres – 24,000 of which was not fully developed. This land would later allow the council to tackle the housing question with vigour once it had accepted the need for municipal housing.

Numbers 3, 4, 5 and 6 in Number 7 Court, Cheapside, about 1905. The girls are chopping firewood and near them is the communal stand pipe providing cold water for everyone in the yard. The brew'us is on the right and the lavatories and shopping at the bottom of the yard.

At its own request, the parish of Quinton was incorporated in to Birmingham in 1909. The following year the council initiated the city's first town-planning scheme under the 1909 Act, and in 1913 it became the first in the country to be accepted by the government. It covered Quinton, Harborne and Edgbaston, and provided the model both for later schemes in areas annexed by the city in 1911 and for other local authorities. The 838 acres of Quinton were mostly undeveloped and the scheme prohibited manufactories, scheduling only residential building. There were three reasons for this: firstly, the absence of railway lines; secondly, because the district lay to the west and prevailing winds would have carried factory smoke over Edgbaston and other middle-class residential districts; and thirdly, because it was a desirable place to live. Two areas each in Harborne and Quinton were set apart for parks and open spaces and not more than twelve houses were to be built per acre. This compared to the eighteen per acre in recently-developed Sparkhill, where there had not been a town-planning scheme. However, whilst the council made nine of Quinton's twenty-three streets, it built none of the houses. The East Birmingham Scheme followed swiftly. Also approved in 1913, it covered 1,443 acres in Saltley, Washwood Heath, Ward End, Little Bromwich and Small Heath. Fifty-one acres were set aside for allotments, but because the districts were downwind and development was aimed at working-class folk, they were to be laid out for factories and houses – the latter at a density of between twelve to eighteen an acre. Again there was no municipal building.

Birmingham's housing question demanded a radical solution, but most councillors still relied on private enterprise for a solution. It did not provide it. Except for the unpopular flats in Hospital and Palmer Streets, private builders conspicuously avoided providing the accommodation required by the poor. By 1913, this failure could be ignored no longer. A special Housing Inquiry Committee was appointed to examine the housing conditions in the poorer parts of the city and advise on policy making. With Nettlefold no longer on the council and the Housing Committee merged with the Health Committee, the inquiry was chaired by Neville Chamberlain. Representing the Liberal Unionists and Conservatives, he was joined amongst others by the Liberal housing reformer, George Cadbury, and by the Independent Labour Councillor, George Shann. The committee's recommendations tended to vindicate Nettlefold's approach of property improvement, piecemeal clearance and town planning in the suburbs. Loathe to spend public money on building houses, it was felt that the slum problem would be resolved by the migration of the working class from the centre to the suburbs. This needed to be encouraged by the council which was advised to buy estates and develop them for house building on town-planning lines. This should be achieved by providing space for public buildings, recreation grounds, and allotments; constructing roads; and laying on gas, water, and electricity mains. Subsequently, the building plots should be leased on low ground rents to private builders who would erect houses subject to restrictions on numbers, character and rental. In this way the better-off workers could move into new homes and the poor could leave their slums and trickle up into the vacated dwellings.

Mrs Janet Buckley and Mrs Isabelle Bailey with their children outside West Lodge flats in Palmer Street, Bordesley, 12 August 1976. (Birmingham Evening Mail*). Erected in 1903, by the 1970s these dwellings were used as half-way house for homeless families. In Janet Buckley's case, she and her family had been put into the flats after they had arrived in Birmingham from Leeds – her husband having obtained an engineering job here. Isabelle Bailey and her husband had been living in a private rented flat but had been evicted when she had her baby. This photograph was taken following a furore caused by Graham Godde, the local housing aid officer for Shelter, who had called for the flats to be closed as sub-standard housing. Families had to share communal bathrooms which often did not work, few repairs were done and mothers had to struggle up stairs with prams and shopping. Within a few years, the flats were closed.*

The Housing Inquiry Committee had the misfortune to tackle the accumulated housing problems caused by 100 years of inaction. Progressive councils highlighted the inertia of nineteenth-century Birmingham. From 1869, Liverpool had embarked upon an ambitious policy of slum clearance and municipal house building. By 1912, an active Conservative council on Merseyside had improved over 11,000 houses, demolished another 5,500 and built 2,322 properties. Similarly, at the end of the 1800s, the London County Council had set upon an impressive slum clearance and municipal house building scheme in Shoreditch. The contrast with Birmingham was glaring. Up to 1913, landlords had reconditioned 3,311 houses, 2,774 had been knocked down, and a meagre 165 council homes had been built in their place. At only 15s (75p) a head compared with £56 a head for Liverpool's policy, slum-patching cost little to ratepayers but it could be only a stop-gap measure. The long-term deterioration of back-to-back housing was not halted, although a decisive solution to the housing question was prevented and a higher cost ensured when a resolute approach was agreed finally. The Housing Inquiry Committee recognised that the council had 'merely played' with the housing problem by building a few houses in Milk Street. Successful municipal housing had to be large scale, but this was a daunting outlook. Birmingham had 43,366 back-to-backs; 42,020 houses without their own water supply; and 58,028 with no separate lavatory. Any rehousing scheme for those living in inadequate housing meant building at least 50,000 houses. This prospect was balked at because of the gigantic cost which would be necessary and the declaration of war in 1914 stifled further discussions.

Women and children living in the Milk Street flats, 1950s. These buildings were demolished in 1966. (Bournville Village Trust).

Before The First World War, the housing question was not just a matter of improving the living conditions of the poor because it was the right and humane thing to do. For many middle-class people, the housing question was inextricably linked to behaviour and they assumed that bad housing fostered bad people. In their misguided opinion, the poor were more prone to drunkenness, violence, over-spending and sexual licentiousness just because they lived in back-to-back houses. The crowding of people in the congested central wards of Birmingham and other big cities was believed to lead to the triumph of the beast in people. Consequently, housing had to be improved if the morals of the poor were to be raised. There was a strong admixture of self-interest and self preservation in this argument of the rich. They feared the poor. By the 1900s the middle-class birth rate had declined sharply whilst that of the poor stayed high: in 1905, in the deprived ward of Deritend, it was 34.9 per thousand, but in Edgbaston it was only 19.7. It was thought that the growing numbers of the poor were a danger to the ruling class. Further, because they were malnourished, they tended to be smaller in physique and were not regarded as good workers or soldiers. Better houses were needed, then, not only for the well-being of the poor but also for the preservation of the social order and of the Empire.

Number 24, Bullock Street, off Windsor Street, Duddeston, about 1905. It looks as if this is a site for Romanies. ('Slum Collection').

The poor lived hidden away from the prosperous. Their narrow streets and labyrinthine courtyards seemed forbidding and unwelcoming. The middle class feared them as unknown territories, sending missionaries to establish mission halls and civilise their inhabitants. Little did they realise that the poor could have taught them much about sharing, helping the needy, and caring for others. Of course, poorer districts had their quota of unkind and dislikeable people, but so too did middle-class areas. Poverty and bad housing did not make the poor inhuman, instead it made them more aware of the needs of each other. Life in a poor locality would have been unbearable without good neighbourliness. Each neighbourhood seemed to have a local 'mother' to whom every one would run for advice if there was sickness or an accident. Poverty meant little money for doctors or undertakers, so other women delivered babies and laid out the dead – at no cost. Communal support was everywhere in a poor neighbourhood, from minding children and granny rearing to lending food and giving sympathy. Pawnbrokers were often friendly, lending more money than an article was worth, and corner shopkeepers threw out a valuable life line with strap. Poverty-stricken neighbourhoods were not slumped in despair – there was friendship as well as offensiveness, laughter as well as sadness. To outsiders they were inhospitable and ought to be erased; to those who belonged, they provided support and made life bearable.

Courtyard in Cromwell Street, Duddeston, about 1905. Notice the matriarchal woman in the foreground with the palings around her patch of land and the plants on her windowsill. Perhaps she is the gaffer of the yard. Once again look at the clean pinnies and lines of washing. The shadow in the middle is a little girl skipping, her movements too fast for the cameras of the day to capture her. Mrs Muckler of Stoke Street, Ladywood wondered 'how we can say they were happy days, but they were. We had never known luxury, so it wasn't missed or craved for, it was the small things in life, the togetherness and love from family life.' ('Slum Collection', Birmingham Library Services).

Chapter 2:

The Era of Council Housing, 1914-1939

The First World War had a tremendous effect on attitudes towards the housing problem. Britain's rulers and prosperous classes had been amazed at the patriotism of the working-class. Men and women had volunteered in their hundreds of thousands to fight and work for a country which had failed the poor and which had given them poverty rather than comfort, ill-health instead of vitality, slum housing in place of decent homes. The realisation dawned that the poor were not a separate race, that they were as much British as were the middle class. Their efforts in contributing to victory had to be recognised and rewarded, and an unwritten social contract evolved that focused on creating a Land Fit for Heroes. The sacrifice of the people was to be matched by a government commitment to major social reforms once the war was ended. Expectations were raised that women would be given the vote, that there would be educational reform, the extension of national insurance, and much else. But the greatest hopes were attached to a solution to the housing problem. Lloyd George, the Prime Minister, and his cabinet recognised that this was the crux of any social reform. They began to plan a housing policy which was to be started once Germany was defeated. It was symbolised by the slogan 'Homes Fit for Heroes'. This swept the land and was taken up by the working class with fervour and eagerness.

Maimed veterans from The First World War at the Central Edgbaston Crown Green Bowling Club, about 1917. (Gerry Hjelter). In 1918, Walter Long, President of the Local Government Board declared that 'to let them (our heroes) come home from horrible, water-logged trenches to something little better than a pigsty here would, indeed, be criminal . . . and a negation of all we have said during the war, that we can never repay those men for what they have done for us'. Two years later, George V stated that decent, sanitary houses must be provided if unrest were to be avoided and a healthy race reared.

Before 1914, housing reformers were motivated by a genuine concern for the distress of the poor, and by a fear that they threatened the social order. For many, better housing was a humanitarian gesture but it was also practical as it would lead to fitter and less discontented workers. Despite the increased emphasis on social concern after 1919, this element of expediency did not disappear from the housing question. During the last year of the war, 41% of conscripts were medically graded as unfit for military service. The future of the nation was believed to be dependent on raising these men, classified as C3, in to the A1 category of fitness and strength. It was felt that decent housing would do this, as well as avoid unrest and improve the 'morals' of the poor. As much as justness then, political judgement made the government aware that urgent action was needed if the housing problem was not to lead to graver social problems. But heroes were returning to even more depressing conditions than they had left. In Birmingham, an investigation revealed that out of 600 discharged soldiers with tuberculosis, no less than 107 were living in dwellings containing two families. Thus, men with an infective disease were sleeping in the same room as their wives and children. The housing problem badly affected many people; it demanded a drastic solution.

Susan and Hyram Flint and their children in the garden of 6 back of 75, Bromsgrove Street – a three storey back-to-back, early 1920s. This is another photograph which emphasises how hard many folk worked to combat the bad conditions they had to endure. (Mrs Mansell).

Whatever its source, the recognition grew that both the state and councils had to be involved actively in solving the housing problem. A decisive shift in attitudes was signified firstly by the formation of an Advisory Housing Panel, and secondly by a Government appeal issued to local authorities in 1917. This made the point that private enterprise would be unable to deal swiftly and successfully with the massive house-building programme which was needed once peace came. By 1918 the wind of change resulted in a momentous transformation of policy. The government agreed to offer substantial financial aid to councils which would undertake municipal house-building, and it accepted the revolutionary recommendations of the Tudor Walters Committee on Working-Class Housing. Building was to be encouraged, but at no more than twelve houses per acre in towns. A minimum of 70 feet should separate opposing houses, so that there could be a proper penetration of light in the winter. Eight was to be the maximum number of dwellings in a block; different styles of housing in the same road were advocated; and wide frontages were advised so as to prevent the construction of narrow but deep, tunnel-back houses. Consequently, long, dreary, parallel terraces were discouraged. Most importantly, the committee believed it essential that each house should have at least a living room, parlour and scullery downstairs, three bedrooms above, and a larder and bathroom. Interestingly, the house plans used in the Bournville Village were endorsed by the Tudor Walters Report. Brighter, more airy, and larger homes were offered as a prospect to the working class. The era of municipal house-building was at hand.

Corner of Kenwood Road, Batchelor's Farm Estate, Bordesley Green, 1926. One thousand three hundred and sixty houses were built here on one of Birmingham's first inter-war estates. (Birmingham Library Services).

Britain's war-time coalition government had assented to the far-reaching and visionary recommendations of the Tudor Walters Report. However, if its advice was to be acted on and the housing problem tackled determinedly, then effective legislation was required speedily. This came with the Housing and Town Planning Act of 1919, also known as the Addison Act after the minister who supervised its introduction. Previous to the First World War, many of the provisions of housing acts were not compulsory, councils implemented them only if they wished to. The Addison Act ended this age of permissive housing legislation, whilst heralding the new policy of municipal house-building aided by the state. For the first time a national act placed on local authorities the responsibility of providing adequate housing for working-class people. Councils were required to find out the need for working-class dwellings in their areas and to provide for it with plans which were to be approved by the Ministry of Health. The government offered financial assistance to limit any losses made by municipalities in excess of a penny rate, thus introducing the principle of support from the state. The better structure and superior amenities planned for the new council houses meant that an economic rent would have placed them beyond the reach of the people they were designed for. Consequently, another significant principle established was that of fixing their rents independently of the costs for their building.

The man with the crutch in the doorway might be a disabled veteran of the Great War, Allison Street, 1920s.

Dreadful housing conditions endured by one Birmingham family, 11 October 1930. (Birmingham Evening Mail).

On a local level, Birmingham reflected the seriousness of the housing problem which had led to fundamental shifts in government policy. The city's normal building requirement was 2,500 new houses each year, but construction had stopped during the war. Consequently, by 1918 there was a pressing housing shortage in Birmingham, exacerbated by a rise in population because of an influx of war workers. Over 12,000 dwellings had to be built immediately to catch up with the back log, and this was without attention to the formidable problems posed by the increasingly run down back-to-backs of the city. Many had been condemned before the war and more had become unfit to live in because they had not been repaired or decorated since 1914. Nearly 200,000 people lived in them – a population as large as Cardiff or Bolton – and the detrimental effect they had on health was illustrated graphically in 1918 by Dr Robertson. He showed that those parts of Birmingham where back-to-backs were most common were the areas where the death rates were at their highest for diarrhoea, measles, bronchitis and pneumonia, and phthisis (wasting disease). They were also the worst districts for infant mortality and their general death rate was twice as high as that of suburban wards. The grimness of the housing situation was realised by the council. In 1917 a new Housing and Town Planning Committee was established and the following year it accepted the government's scheme of encouraging municipal building. It became obvious that the answer to the housing problem was to be found in a partnership between local and national authorities.

In 1917 the council's Public Health Committee had called the attention of the Housing Committee to the depressing contrast between the health of the people of the various areas of Birmingham. The opinion was held that the high sickness and mortality rates in the central wards called for a radical improvement in the housing conditions of those districts. However, because of the housing shortage in the city, the measures needed to remedy the problem could not be taken until there was a considerable addition made to the number of working-class dwellings. The Housing Committee was requested earnestly to give the subject their earliest possible consideration and soon it acquired 400 acres of land for building. Still, it was not until the passing of the Addison Act that a coherent and effective housing policy could be contemplated. Consequently, Birmingham council set up a Housing and Estates Department with a regular committee and a Housing Director as a full-time official. His brief was to plan and supervise the building of municipal estates; to manage them; and to collect the rents. Unfortunately, his job was made burdensome by severe post-war difficulties. There were shortages of materials and of labour – especially bricklayers – and there was controversy over the employment of private contractors, instead of direct labour, to build council houses. Still, it was hoped that a vigorous programme of rehousing in the suburbs would solve the problems of the central wards.

A woman and child are in the brew'us in a yard at the back of Florence Street, off Bath Row, 1930s. To the right of the old lady is a maiding tub, in which the washing was banged clean, and a scrubbing tub. Both were made out of one barrel. Behind the lady is the mangle. (Sylvia Leigh).

The new Housing Manager was faced with a severe crisis. Birmingham's population had increased, new building had ceased, and there were around 40,000 back-to-backs needing to be cleared and their tenants rehoused. Five thousand homes had to be built each year for the next twenty years if the city's housing problem was to be tackled successfully. Despite difficulties with labour and materials, a start was made quickly on providing the new council dwellings needed so desperately. By the end of 1919 tenants were moved in to the corporation houses in Cotterills Lane, Alum Rock – the first occupied under the new building programme. Other dwellings were built at Billesley Farm (Kings Heath), Pineapple Farm (Stirchley) Stonehouse Farm (California), and elsewhere. In all, 3,234 houses were erected under the 1919 scheme. All were of a good construction and in terms of space they were the best built by the council between the wars. They were fitted with dressers and cupboards; supplied with gas lighting; and had a separate bathroom. Nearly 3,000 were of the 3B type, that is they had a living room, parlour, scullery, and three bedrooms. Unlike much council housing later, this design reflected the wishes of prospective tenants. It was based on the recommendations of the Tudor Walters Report which had listened to groups like the Women's Labour League. These bodies had indicated the preference of working-class people for a parlour and living room rather than a through lounge. Such a style meant that families could have the symbol of respectability – a front room 'for best'.

Newly-built council houses in Stechford, mid 1920s. Cotterills Lane is on the left. Notice the muddy road and unpaved footpaths. (Birmingham Library Services).

By 1922, agricultural land was widely falling under the sway of urbanisation and new residential areas had been formed by the council in Birchfield, Bordesley Green, Bournville, California, Erdington, Gospel Oak, Kings Heath, Little Bromwich, Quinton, Short Heath, Stechford, Stirchley and Warstock. With the swift and ongoing expansion in the numbers of municipal dwellings, the Housing and Estates Department decided their new tenants needed advice on maintaining their homes and estates in a respectable fashion. With funds from the Common Good Trust, a monthly publication was launched. Called the *Municipal Tenants Monthly* it encouraged gardening on council estates, distributed useful information to tenants, and tried to foster a spirit of neighbourliness amongst them. The efforts behind the magazine were well-intentioned but artificial, and it was short-lived. Yet tenants themselves did recognise the need for communal action on estates where the housing was good but in which facilities were lacking. Various groups were formed – like the association for gardening on the Linden Road Estate and the tenants' association on the Pineapple Estate. This latter aimed to protect tenants' interests; to co-operatively buy seeds and plants; to hire out gardening tools and books; to arrange lectures; and to pass on complaints to the Housing Department. Its representations led to the erection of a letter box and a public telephone box on the estate and its actions indicated the importance of pressure by tenants in order to establish essential facilities.

A horse-drawn cart belonging to E.O.C. Howells, one of the contractors responsible for these council houses in Chinnbrook Road on the Billesley Estate, 1926. (Victor Pugh). Notice the brickie at work on the scaffolding and the other worker by the ladder on the right. That year, Councillor Griffiths told the Billesley Tenants Magazine *that when he first visited the district in October 1920 'the difficulty was to find the Electors, in many cases there was half a mile or more between the houses'. Now the most striking fact was 'the remarkable change which has come over Billesley and Yardley Wood. In place of hundreds of acres of agricultural land and half-a-dozen farms the area is covered by more than two thousand houses.'*

"As our garden was a field only nine months ago, there are many ways in which I can help Daddy. The ground is full of stones; so these have to be dug out, and be placed on the path where Daddy will dig them in. Then I can keep off the edge of the lawn until it is properly set. I can keep the tools clean and oiled; and when Daddy wants them, get them out; and put them back when finished with. When Daddy was making the arches over the path, I held the branches for him. Whenever I see manure on the road, I get it for the marrow bed. Then there are seeds to plant; while Daddy makes the holes, I hold, and put into the holes, potatoes, etc. We also have a bird-table where waste scraps and crumbs are put; this I keep supplied." (Herbert Wallace Litten, age 12 years, Brook Lane, *Kings Heath Municipal Tenants Monthly,* 1922).

Gardens are prominent in this shot of Marston Road, Weoley Castle, 1930s. Mrs Clift's mom and dad were amongst the first tenants in nearby Kemberton Road, Weoley Castle, having moved from Brearley Street, Summer Lane neighbourhood. It had 'a lovely garden back and front and plenty of fresh air . . . The back garden joined on to farm land where cows used to come to the fence'. Birmingham's 40,000th council house built since 1919 was at 30, Hopstone Road, Weoley Castle. On the occasion of its completion, Neville Chamberlain, then Chancellor of the Exchequer, declared that Birmingham had achieved something 'which has no parallel in this or any other country'.

Originally, Birmingham council had intended to erect 10,000 houses under the 1919 Act but its construction programme was beset by problems and it failed to reach its target by nearly 6,000 dwellings. A major reason for this shortfall was the soaring cost of building nationally which led to an average price of £1,000 for Addison houses. Those built in Birmingham cost between £900 and £1,000 each – about four times the pre-war level. Spiralling expenses were not unique to the city. The unlimited government subsidy beyond the figure of a penny rate encouraged profiteering by some builders and extravagance by certain local authorities. As the brief post-war boom turned swiftly into depression, the government decided that no longer could it afford to subsidise municipal house-building. In 1921 construction costs reached their climax and this provided the opportunity for the state to limit its liability. The Addison Act fell victim to the notorious 'Geddes Axe' which stopped all new approvals for building programmes. This resulted in a significant slowing down in the construction activities of local authorities. Runaway expenditure came at an opportune time for those who opposed public involvement in the provision of homes for working-class people. Many expressed the hope that the building industry would return to its pre-war economic basis. This meant a withdrawal of involvement by the state and a reliance on private enterprise to supply the housing needs of newly-weds and slum dwellers.

The wedding of Marjorie and Fred Luckett of Aston, 1920s. (Arthur Wilkes).

Once again, the national debate on the housing question was mirrored in Birmingham. From its inception in 1919, critics had attacked the Housing and Town Planning Committee as slow, inefficient, wasteful and ill-advised. Controversy over its activities increased, and although from November 1919 it had a preponderance of Labour councillors, the disapproval of the committee's activities was not fully a political issue. Its first chairman, George Cadbury, was a Liberal and he was followed by Siward James, a Conservative. Indeed, the highly censorious *Evening Mail* emphasised that reactions against the committee should not be regarded as demonstrations against Labour Party ideals or methods. Eventually, the storm of censure led the council to set up a Special Committee of Inquiry into the workings of the Housing Committee. Its report, published in 1922, was highly critical of inexperienced officials, of the lack of careful supervision of housing contracts, of friction with builders, and of ill-feeling with the Public Works Committee which was responsible for roads and drainage works. With hindsight, much of the condemnation seems unfair. The Ministry of Health was urging councils to build good quality houses, whilst Birmingham had a severe housing problem and exorbitant building prices were a national difficulty. The most relevant criticism was of the unwise purchase of estates which were distant from the city and which had neither roads or drainage. Consequently, they were costly to develop and this increased expense led to the building of fewer houses than had been planned.

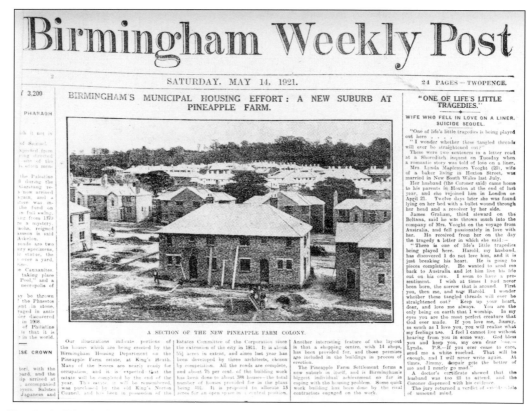

Headline in the Birmingham Weekly Post *about the new suburb emerging at the Pineapple Farm Estate, Stirchley, 14 May 1921. In the* Municipal Tenants Monthly *in 1922 a correspondent called 'Jud' described his joy when 'we found ourselves modern houses, with hot and cold water laid on . . . with gardens awaiting cultivation, and then full of promise and reward. We found convenience for coal storage in the dry, without cartage through the house; we found back and front entrances installed; suitable washing and bathroom accommodation was a fully appreciated point; not to mention the airing cupboard upstairs. Then, did we appreciate burglar-proof non-falling windows, or mice-proof cement halls and kitchens, design of structure for gas stove?'*

Following the adverse report on its activities, in April 1922 the Housing Committee put forward a statement as to its future policy. One thousand eight hundred houses had been built up to that date, but the committee still had on its books 10,000 applicants and believed it would have more if people had any hope of obtaining a home. Consequently, it wanted to make representations to the Ministry of Health to build more dwellings under the assisted houses scheme, bringing them up to a total of 6,000. However, the sustained assault on its actions since 1919 took its toll. The hostile publicity continued, three members of the Housing Committee resigned, and it was felt by many councillors that insufficient attention had been taken of the charges laid against it. Alderman Sir David Brooks had headed the Special Inquiry Committee and he proposed that there would be a more speedy and economical building of houses if the responsibility for construction under the state-assisted scheme be transferred from the Housing and Estates Committee. After a long and animated debate this proposal was carried by 53 votes to 34. As a result, the newly-named Public Works and Town Planning Committee became responsible for building council houses, whilst an Estates Committee took over responsibility for the management of corporation estates and the allocation of houses on them to applicants.

The Estates Department, Summer Lane, 1933. On display are prize winners from the council's popular gardening competitions.

Opponents of the Housing Committee declared that they were not against council house-building, but their victory did echo the national resurgence of support for private builders. The Public Works Committee was in favour of private enterprise whenever possible, a feeling shared by the Conservative minister responsible for housing policy, Neville Chamberlain MP for Birmingham Ladywood. His solution to the national housing problem imitated the city's long-held faith in the private sector as the agent of housing reform. Accordingly, the 1923 Housing Act aimed to stimulate private development, revive the building trade and accelerate the erection of dwellings. Councils were encouraged to lend money to enable private purchase of homes; building societies were supported in making mortgages easier; and a subsidy was provided for both dwellings built by local authorities and private builders. However, an annual grant of £6 per house for twenty years was the most that councils could claim, and they could only build if the Minister was convinced that it would be better for them to do so than private enterprise. As a result of a general fall in prices, and because of the sudden reduction in demand for building after the 'Geddes Axe', construction costs fell sharply to about half their previous level. Yet the new subsidy was not large enough to revive municipal house-building on a large scale. Those living in insanitary dwellings still awaited an extensive housing programme to improve their lives.

Reg Whitehouse and sister Gert outside their council house at 14, Springthorpe Road, Pype Hayes, a contrast to their former house at 34, Trafalgar Road, opposite Spring Hill, Erdington which had been lit by gas, early 1930s. (Reg Whitehouse).

Chamberlain's approach led to a complete reversal in the policy of encouraging local authorities to become the main providers of houses for working-class people, but it did invigorate the private sector. In Birmingham private builders had erected only 382 houses in 1922; in 1924 they built 1,201. Undoubtedly, their renewed interest was stimulated by the council's decision to pass on, in a lump sum of £75, the grant provided by the Act. The city itself added another £25, giving a total subsidy to private builders of £100 per house. This was subject to a maximum selling price of £600 freehold, exclusive of the subsidy. In 1927 a reduction in the annual government grant led the council to drop its lump sum subsidy to £50, and the following year the scheme ended when the state abandoned the grant altogether. Not only was the council influential in lowering the price of houses built by private enterprise, it also instituted a progressive mortgage scheme. This helped people who wished to build dwellings by granting them loans on advantageous terms. The amount advanced represented about 90% of the value of the house when completed, payable in instalments as the building proceeded. This scheme terminated in 1931 after the building of 1,377 dwellings. Overall, average three-bedroom houses without a parlour had fallen in building costs from £930 in August 1920, to £436 in March 1922. This drop and the availability of easier mortgages from 1923, enabled a few highly-paid members of the working class to buy their own homes. Nevertheless, home-buying remained unattainable for the vast majority of working-class families.

A mother with her toddler daughter chatting with an old lady at the entrance to Court 36 in Woodcock Street, near Gosta Green, 1930s.

To try and extend home ownership to the working class, the council introduced an exciting scheme enabling corporation tenants to buy their property. The subsidy under Chamberlain's Act was passed on to the purchaser; mortgages were provided by the Birmingham Municipal Bank; and the Estates Department handled sales, publishing a booklet in 1925 called, *How to be Your Own Landlord*. It divided the city in to five districts, although no municipal houses were for sale in the central area. Corporation dwellings built specifically for purchase were available in Acocks Green, Alum Rock, Bordesley Green, Billesley, Erdington, Fox Hollies, Hay Mills, Kings Heath, Pype Hayes, Short Heath, Small Heath and Ward End. By 1929, when the subsidy was discontinued, more than £1,000,000 had been loaned by the Municipal Bank to buyers of 3,314 council houses. In 1925 an end or semi-detached parlour-type home in Foxton Road, Alum Rock, cost £468, with £448 for a middle house. An end or semi-detached non parlour-type house in Brookvale Park Road, Erdington, cost £338, with £317 for a middle house. The house purchasing scheme was adventurous and innovative but home ownership did remain a daunting prospect. A house in Ilford Road, Short Heath cost £372 to buy in 1925, plus £3 6s (30p) legal fees. If a £20 deposit was paid and £352 borrowed over twenty years at 5% interest, the tenant needed to find 13s (65p) weekly in repayments, plus 6s (30p) for rates, ground rent and insurance. This compared to an inclusive council rent of 11s 2d (56p) – and even this was still a fifth of an average working man's wage.

Margaret Causer (nee Keight) is the tall girl with her brothers and sisters in Steel Grove, of Kathleen Road, Yardley, about 1932. (Margaret Causer).

Unsurprisingly, a Conservative government had encouraged home ownership. Easier mortgages, government subsidies and falling building costs allowed many lower middle-class people to buy their own houses for the first time. In Birmingham, the local Conservative party was reliant on widespread working-class support for its council majority and so it was more sensitive than the national party to the needs of upper working-class families. Consequently, it had made a determined attempt to enable them to buy their properties. Yet, neither private purchase nor council house building catered for most working-class people, let alone the huge numbers of poor living in back-to-backs. The Public Works Committee acknowledged this and though staunchly in favour of private enterprise it confessed, that at least in the short term, the council had to build as many houses as possible. In 1922 it reported that the 1919 Act had not solved the city's housing problem. Indeed, at just over a third of the annual average before 1906, house-building was not even providing for Birmingham's normal growth in population. Furthermore, the rent of municipal dwellings was too dear for the average working-class family, let alone the poor. This damning indictment of national housing policy led the council to instruct the committee to erect as many houses as possible in the next two years – even without government approval or financial assistance; and to acquire and develop building estates subject to a financial loss of no more than a 3d (1½p) rate.

A view of Glebe Street, November 1936. Under Greenwood's Act of 1936, this street was cleared and disappeared. A pudding bag street, cul-de-sac, it had run between Rawlins Street and Ladywood Terrace. Many houses were demolished during the interwar years, but as in the late nineteenth centuries such action was piecemeal. The clearance of Glebe Street is a rare example in Birmingham of more comprehensive clearance before the 1950s.

The Public Works and Town Planning Committee preferred private enterprise. It recognised that the building of smaller villas for sale would help the lower middle class directly, but it argued that indirectly the working class would benefit. This would be achieved by a filtering up process. Home buyers would vacate their rented accommodation which would be occupied by the better-paid of the working class. In turn, their former houses would be rented by the poor, leaving the back-to-backs of the city abandoned. In this way, all Brummies would naturally and easily move in to better housing. This policy took no account of the inability of the poor to afford to rent dwellings other than back-to-backs, it paid no attention to their need to live near the available work, and it ignored the pull of communal loyalty and neighbourhood support. Utopian in thought and impracticable, it could never have solved Birmingham's housing problem. To its credit, the committee ditched its principles and recognised that it was of outstanding importance for the council to build small houses for rent. Indeed, in 1923 it erected 1,508 dwellings, whereas 970 had been the highest annual total built under the Housing and Town Planning Committee. Still, this rate of building was not enough. By 1925 it was estimated that there was a shortage of 30,000 dwellings in Birmingham; there were 24,840 applicants for new housing registered with the Estates Department; and overcrowding had increased in poorer areas. Many more new houses were needed desperately. They could be provided only if central government assisted councils with subsidies.

Ted Reynolds outside his family's council house at 4, Eastlands Road, Moseley, about 1927. (Ted Reynolds). When she was ten, Mrs Malyn's family moved to nearby Yardley Wood from Heath Mill Lane, Deritend: 'about 6 months before we moved in the previous tenant had the gas mantle taken out and electric installed. As you may know we were in a new world. The toilet was still outside but our own.'

By the mid 1920s the shortage of working-class houses was greater than it had been in 1919 when the boast of 'Homes Fit for Heroes' echoed across the land. Coming to power in 1924 the first Labour government was determined to tackle this housing crisis. Wheatley, the new Minister of Health, introduced a Housing Act and tilted the balance back in favour of municipal building. The subsidy on new dwellings was increased to £9 per house for forty years – on condition that local authorities also made an annual grant of not more than £4.10s (50p) per house. Subsidised homes had to be let, not sold; the benefit of the subsidy was to be passed on to tenants by reducing rents; and local authorities were to build their houses to the same standards laid down in Chamberlain's Act. This had promoted the building of non-parlour type homes with a bathroom, a policy advocated by Birmingham's Public Works and Town Planning Committee in 1922. Such homes were smaller than those with a parlour, but on average they were £50 less to construct and consequently more could be built at a lower rent. Obviously, tenants preferred a larger house with a parlour, but their costliness prevented them being a realistic answer to the massive housing shortage. The only viable solution to the housing shortage was the erection of large numbers of non-parlour homes at no more than twelve houses per acre. Although the amount of subsidy varied between 1924 and 1933, the Wheatley Act was the catalyst for a huge expansion in council house-building.

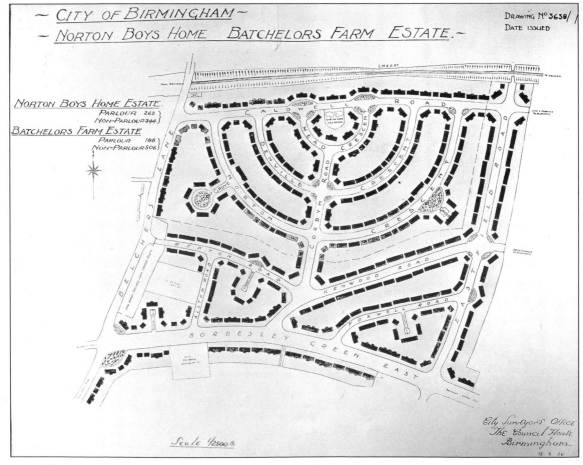

Plan of the Batchelor's Farm Estate, Bordesley Green. The groves and crescents indicate the influence of town planners on the lay out of inter-war corporation estates and show the rejection of 'Coronation-Street' style roads of long terraces so common in the developments of house builders before 1914.

For fifty years Birmingham Council had believed that private enterprise would provide the answer to the city's dreadful housing problem. It was proven wrong. The realisation of this mistake came slowly, but once apparent the council enthusiastically adopted a programme of municipal house-building as encouraged by the Wheatley Act. The transformation in policy was astounding. In 1924, the year the act was passed, the city erected 1,663 houses; in 1925 this figure increased dramatically to 3,066. The same year the *Birmingham Gazette* reported that, on average, six houses per hour were being completed at the Batchelor's Farm Estate, Bordesley Green. In 1930 alone – the peak year of council house-building before 1939 – 6,715 corporation houses were erected. Indeed, on 25 July 1930, Arthur Greenwood, Labour's Minister of Health, opened Birmingham's 30,000th council house in the appropriately-named Greenwood Place, Kingstanding. By 1933, when the Wheatley Act ceased operation, 33,612 corporation homes had been erected under its provisions, compared to only 3,433 under Chamberlain's Act. Birmingham had built more council houses than any other local authority in England. This success was due to a remarkable partnership between a Labour government and a Conservative led council supported in its housing policy by Labour representatives. The depression of the 1930s led to a slowing down in council house-building, but in 1939 the 50,000th council house in the city was opened at Fellmeadow Road, Lea Hall. Rightly, Conservative and Labour councillors congratulated themselves on an achievement unique in the history of English local government. Overall, between 1919 and 1939, the corporation constructed 51,681 houses. This compared to 59,744 privately-built dwellings. The two sectors together allowed the rehousing of 200,000 people – one fifth of Birmingham's population.

Private houses in Ingestre Road, Hall Green, 1930s. (Carl Thomas Collection). Like many outer city areas built up during the inter-war years, Hall Green had a large council estate, the Gospel Oak and Pitmaston, as well as significant developments for owner occupiers.

Ingestre Road, Stratford Road, Hall Green.

The enlarged Birmingham of 1911 numbered 840,000 people; by 1931 the figure had increased considerably to 1,000,000. This overall rise disguised significant internal movements of population which indicated that a steady decentralisation was in process. Between 1921 and 1931 the number of people in the central wards of Birmingham declined from 242,000 to about 188,000 – a shrinkage of 22.5%. There was a similar decrease in population in the middle ring wards, from 380,000 to around 288,000 – a drop of 24.1%. In contrast to these falls, there was a massive increase in the people living in the outer ring wards. Their population rose from 300,000 in 1921 to about 571,000 by 1931 – a massive 91% expansion. Obviously, a major factor in this phenomenal growth was the building of new council estates in districts which had joined the city in 1911 and afterwards. Not all the incorporated areas grew in numbers. Aston had much in common with the central wards of the old city – it was mostly built up, and many of its houses were back-to-backs; and Handsworth too, was largely developed. By comparison, although Erdington, Kings Norton, Northfield and Yardley were expanding rapidly, they contained farmland ripe for development. So too, did Quinton; Perry Barr, added to the city in 1928; and Sheldon, included within the boundaries 1931. It was in these districts that the majority of council estates were built in the inter-war years. Often, the only link they retained with their rural past was in their names – such as Glebe Farm, Gospel Farm, Billesley Farm and Pineapple Farm.

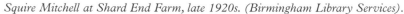

Squire Mitchell at Shard End Farm, late 1920s. (Birmingham Library Services).

The planners of the new estates were determined that they should differ significantly from the middle ring wards developed by private enterprise before 1919. Here, miles of tunnel-back houses lined tree-less, straight roads in a 'Coronation-Street' fashion. Areas like Small Heath, Sparkhill and Bournbrook were an improvement on the dismal central wards but they did not inspire enthusiasm in the supporters of the garden-city idea. The countryside had been banished from them, there were too many houses to the acre, and their long rows of terraced dwellings were regarded as soulless and monotonous. Birmingham's inter-war council estates reflected the distaste of town planner's for uniformity, but cost prevented them from emerging as ideal garden cities. They were characterised by a complex geometric pattern of straight roads, circles and crescents. Building was mostly twelve houses per acre, occasionally fifteen; houses were erected in blocks of two, four or six – so breaking up frontage lines; and all had front and back gardens. Dwellings lay back twenty feet or more from tree lined roads and they were interspersed by small, open sites. On the earlier large municipal estates, the houses varied little in design, but their layout was different and many natural features of the area were retained. As development progressed, the newer estates showed an improvement in architecture and site layout.

Bye-law housing in Oldfield Road, Sparkbrook. This had developed mostly in the late 1880s and early 1890s when the district had come under the Balsall Heath Local Board of Health (incorporated into Birmingham with Saltley, Harborne, Ward End and Little Bromwich in 1891). The local bye-laws stated that the walls had to be nine inches thick, that is, two bricks thick and effectively disallowing one brick deep back-to-backs. Ten builders were involved in constructing the resulting tunnel backs. This photograph shows Oldfield Road decorated for the silver jubilee of George V. Seated on the doorstep of her house at number 41 is Mrs Jessie Jones. Just in front of her is Mrs Nellie Fisher with two friends from Woodfield Road, Mr Bednall in the cloth cap and Mrs Kinsey. (Mrs N. E. Jones daughter-in-law of Jessie and daughter of Nellie).

Whatever the design of a council estate, there is little doubt that the provision of open spaces and the closeness to farm land were great attractions to working-class people. Children especially delighted in the fresh air and the freedom of wandering and playing in parks and the countryside. In the summer those living at Perry Common Estate earned 6d ($2\frac{1}{2}$p) a day helping with haymaking and potato picking. The contrast was stark with the older, treeless and grassless parts of Birmingham. In 1941 it was found that just over 1% of the area of the central wards was given over to parks or recreation grounds. This compared to nearly 5% in the middle ring and 8.5% in the outer ring. The National Playing Fields Association had suggested a standard of six acres of playing fields per 1,000 people, and this was apart from parks and other open spaces. The ratio in the central wards was an appalling .2; in the middle ring it was 1.6; and in the outer ring it was 5.8. Gardens, too, were largely absent from the poorer parts of Birmingham, with only a third of families having them compared to 96% in the new estates. Middle-class observers waxed lyrical about the sweet breeze from the Vale of Evesham blowing its uncontaminated fragrance over Billesley, giving health and vigour to its inhabitants. Though overstated, it is unlikely that working-class people would have disagreed too much with the sentiments.

The crowded scene in the Lawford Street Recreation Ground, off Vauxhall Road, 1928. Notice how the younger kids are minded by big brothers and sisters. (Birmingham Recreation and Community Services).

" **I**n 1939, my parents arranged an exchange with someone who wanted to live in this area (Hockley) for some unknown reason, for a house on a wonderful new council estate at Perry Common. We therefore went to live at 24 Dovedale Road. It had a long garden, the bottom of which was a stream ... and then there were beautiful open fields right up to Oscott College, and we could also see the observatory. I was not used to such open spaces, and my mother became very worried after a time, because I would not venture to the bottom of the garden, however, after a period of making friends and becoming used to the open spaces I was very happy indeed living there."

(Norman Fearn, Hockley and Perry Common)

" **I**remember if you stood on tip-toe and looked in a certain direction you could just see the top of a tree."

(Mrs Woodfield, Bridge Street West, Hockley)

A Wacaden (Wathes, Cattell and Gurden) dairy float outside inter-war council housing, probably late 1920s.

The accommodation of the new corporation homes was a distinct improvement on that which most tenants had been used to in privately-rented property. They were all fitted with dressers and cupboards, and after 1923 they were provided with electric lighting not gas. Each had a gas ring and gas heating for the washing copper, whilst parlour-type homes had a hot water circulating system. Other less essential features added to the appeal of the houses – perhaps a mantelpiece over the fire place or picture rails around the walls. Under the Chamberlain and Wheatley Acts most of the municipal houses which were built were of the non-parlour variety – nearly 29,000 out of a total of almost 37,000. The majority of these had a hall, large living room, scullery, bathroom which opened out of the scullery, lavatory, coal shed, larder and three bedrooms. There was a smaller non-parlour type which had similar accommodation but less floor area; and a version which had just two bedrooms. Even this was vastly better than a back-to-back which had no bathroom, washing copper or lavatory, and which had only a living room, cellar, two bedrooms, and a tiny scullery containing a black iron stove and a brown crock sink. There was little romantic about fetching coal from a damp, unlighted cellar, or in washing in the brew 'us in the dark and cold of a winter's night.

Alice Brooks with her children Billy and Sylvia in a yard at the back of Bishop Street, by the markets, about 1935. A maid (dolly) used for banging the washing clean is hanging up behind them in the brew'us. (Beryl Brooks).

"At the top of the yard in Barker Street where we lived were two houses facing the entry into the street. In between the two houses was the wash house or 'brew 'us' where the women did their washing. They kept to their own side, one wringer or 'mangle' on one wall and the other opposite. There was no 'free for all', every family kept to their own limits."

(Mrs Piper, Barker Street, Ladywood)

"Wash day was usually on a Monday which was done in the brewhouse up the yard where wood and coal were used to boil up water for the washing. It was my job to start the fire and fill the boiler. I have watched my mother scrubbing collars and boiler suits till 10 o'clock at night. She used to take in washing for other people who paid her about 1s 9d a bundle."

(Mrs Scott, Carver Street, Hockley)

Women mangling outside the brew'us in Court Number 12, Cecil Street, Summer Lane neighbourhood, 1930s. (Sylvia Leigh).

Commentators were fulsome in their praise of the new council estates. They were cleaner, brighter and closer to the country than the central and middle wards; the houses were better-built and equipped with 'up-to-date' facilities; and they possessed gardens encouraging tenants to grow flowers and vegetables. Certainly, these features were appreciated by working-class people, but increasingly they realised that there was a lack of facilities on the new estates. In 1932 a comparison was made between Kingstanding, with about 30,000 people, and the slightly smaller Shrewsbury. The older Shropshire town had thirty churches, fifteen church halls and parish rooms, five other halls, two public libraries, four picture houses and 159 public houses. Kingstanding was a glaring contrast in the provision of communal services. It boasted only one church, one hall, one picture house and one pub, and it had no parks, sports grounds, or hospital. An experimental community centre was planned by the council in 1930 but it was abandoned because of the financial crisis following the Wall Street Crash. Consequently, local people organised themselves and opened the Perrystanding Community Centre off Kingstanding Circle in 1932. Soon after, a sports' ground in Cooksey Lane was acquired and in 1934 a branch of the Summer Lane Settlement was opened. On other estates it was a similar story. At Witton Lodge, a Salvation Army building was used as a centre; and at Gospel Oak a charity had erected a community hall. The first council-funded community centre was not actually opened until 1936. It was provided in Billesley at the junction of Trittiford and Chinnbrook Roads.

The development of Kingstanding Council Estate. Oscott College is on the hill in the background. (Birmingham Library Services). Hilda Hughes and her family moved from Aston to Kingstanding, where 'it was awfully cold . . . in the winter, it was called Little Russia and it was said that if you could live there you could live anywhere. The house was a non parlour council house and I think the rent was about 10/- (50p).

The Billesley Bus Service

Attend all folks who in Billesley dwell,
Whilst I of the bus service do tell.
You who breathe sweet breezes from Evesham's Vale,
And feel the force of the south west gale.

You all remember the time, do you not?
When the roads where rough and a dirty lot.
No buses to carry you near or far,
And you had to walk and your pleasure to mar.

All the kiddies had a terrible time,
Through the rain, and the mud and the slime.
To Dennis Road and Colmore Road they tramped,
And sat all day in clothes that were well damped.

Some trotted north to the number four tram;
Some crossed the fields to get to Birmingham.
Bad were the means of reaching the City,
You aroused the BTA Committee.

The single-man bus came to relieve us,
After much talk and after much fuss.
And we like herrings in a box did ride,
To business and school without much pride.

Down Stoney Lane to the Stratford Road end,
No farther on the bus to depend.
In queue each morning we stood like sheep,
And heard many growls both loud and deep.

The BTA up a petition drew,
Signed by a thousand and a few.
This to the Council did Dalton present,
For a through bus and all that it meant.

Now Billesley has a bus of its own,
From small things it all has grown.
With ease to the City's heart we can ride,
And smile with joy at the whole world wide.

Hurrah! for all the BTA has done,
For you and for me and for everyone.
In its cap it has put a feather fine,
Long may its sun continue to shine.

(*WW, The Billesley Tenants Association Magazine, 1922*)

Trittiford Road School, Billesley, 1932. (Billesley School)

Inevitably, the rapid development of council estates meant that the building of houses outran the provision of facilities for the new population. Tenants' associations, the council and charitable organisations made serious attempts to provide for the deficiency of telephone boxes, libraries, banks and much else. In particular the need for community halls was addressed by the Birmingham Council for Community Associations for the New Housing Estates. Yet by 1936, when one in six Brummies lived in these areas, only five estates had a community hall: Allen's Cross, Billesley, Glebe Farm, Kingstanding and Weoley Castle. The provision of schools also lagged behind the erection of houses and a burgeoning population. Development at Billesley had begun in 1919, but not until 1925 was a school opened in Trittiford Road. Even then it was insufficient for the number of children in the district and although it was built for 400 children a total of 600 were in attendance. An extension was planned to open in October 1926, giving an extra 400 places, but fifteen to twenty families were moving to the locality each week. So great was the number of children waiting to join the school that it could only take those aged between five and nine. Older children would still have to attend a school outside the district, most travelling to Colmore Road in Kings Heath, or Dennis Road in Sparkbrook. Naturally, parents were annoyed at what seemed a lack of co-ordination between the Estates Committee, which managed the estate, and the Education Committee, which provided schools. Much of this disjunction between departments was unavoidable, but it rankled nevertheless.

Party celebrating the silver jubilee of King George V in Firbeck Grove, Kingstanding, 1935. (Mrs Hemming).

Despite the importance of community centres and schools, they were not the most pressing need for many council tenants. They identified quick and cheap transport to and from the city as an urgent priority. At three miles distance, Batchelor's Farm was the nearest estate to town, whilst Allen's Cross, Kingstanding and Lea Hall were five miles away. Although Pype Hayes adjoined an industrial area, few estates had any significant local employment. The huge Stechford Ward included the Lea Hall and Glebe Farm estates, but in 1938 it provided work for only two out of three of its inhabitants. In contrast, the central wards contained only a fifth of Birmingham's population but provided work for over a third. Accordingly, many workers had to make dear and lengthy journeys to their jobs. It cost 10d (4p) and took nearly an hour for a return journey to town from Kingstanding, and from Allen's Cross two buses had to be caught. The Billesley Tenants' Association cited the case of a family rehoused in the district after their home in Aston was condemned. Previously, three of its members had walked to their jobs in Erdington, but now each had to travel six or seven miles at the cost, between them, of 21s (£1 05p) a week. Unsurprisingly, they wished they were back in Aston, even if it were in a dilapidated house. Angered by the swiftness of providing a bus service for middle-class Handsworth Wood, the association campaigned strongly for a direct bus route to the city centre and for workmen's fares. Their lobbying succeeded late in 1925.

Last day of tram service on the Stechford route, 2 December 1948. On the right can be seen council housing on the corner of Bordesley Green East and Kenwood Road. (Mr L. W. Perkins).

Higher travelling costs were not the only drawbacks to living in a better house in a bright new estate. Not until 1929, ten years after council house-building began in earnest, did the council begin to erect shops for letting on estates. Ninety were built before the policy was abandoned in 1932 under pressure from the Conservative-dominated National government which believed that private enterprise should supply the need for retail units. Certainly, shops were opening up on the estates and shopping centres like Erdington, Kings Heath and Northfield were emerging as rivals to those long-established in the central and middle wards. Indeed, the slow decline of the Gooch Street, Ladypool Road and High Street Aston shopping centres dates from the 1920s. Still, although distant these thoroughfares remained extremely popular with council tenants. For one thing they had more shops offering a greater variety of services. Monday morning buses from Kingstanding were known as pawn shop specials, because they carried so many women with their pawn bundles to pawnbrokers in Aston. Saturday's buses, too, were full as women went shopping to the older centres where food was cheaper and bargains could be found as butchers auctioned off their meat as night fell. The price of a tram fare could be recouped easily, but more than economics was involved in these trips. The Ladypool Road and its ilk were familiar, lively, and exciting, with their market-like flavour, bustle and characters.

The bustling scene on the Coventry Road, Small Heath in August 1952. The buses are heading out of town and notice the horse-drawn milk float ahead of the van belonging to Bryant's the builders. On the left is Barklays furnishers on the corner of Chapman Road. (Johnny Landon). The 'Cov' was the artery of Small Heath, as was each of the shopping thoroughfares of working-class Brum. Mrs Curtis of Chesterton Road captured their vitality in evoking the Ladypool Road: 'There was everything down there. One of the finest shopping centres in Birmingham. It was a real good class shopping centre. You could get anything you wanted. All reasonable in price. Plenty of butchers' shops, hucksters' shops. You had pork butchers, offal shops, tripe shops … Wonderful shops.'

A yard in Hospital Street, Summer Lane neighbourhood, 1920s. (COPEC). Mrs Nicholson came from Hospital Street where the rent in the family home had been about 4s 6d (22¹/₂) a week. When they moved to a new municipal house in Yardley Wood the rent rose to 11s 4d (57p).

Higher travelling costs and dearer food were influential in dissuading some people from renting a council house. Undoubtedly, however, the greatest disadvantage of living in a newer, larger and more healthy home was its cost. The rental of a municipal dwelling was too high for poor people, even with the government subsidy and the amount allowed by the corporation under the housing acts. In 1933, the average weekly rent – inclusive of rates – for a parlour house was 15s 6d (77¹/₂p) a week; for a non-parlour type; 11s 4d (57p); and for smaller non-parlour houses, 8s 6d (42¹/₂p) and 10s (50p). At this level, one Birmingham councillor felt that not even a corporation employee with three children could afford to pay the rents except if he deprived his family of necessities. By 1941 the highest rent for municipal houses was 20s (£1) a week, and the lowest was 7s 3d (36p) giving an average of 10s (50p) for a three-bedroom non-parlour dwelling. By comparison, 41% of workers in the central wards were paying less than 8s (40p) a week in rent, and 71% were paying under 10s (50p) weekly. Together, the increased amount of rents, travel and shopping meant that the average working-class family in the suburbs had a cost of living 10% to 15% higher than a similar family living in one of the central wards. In these circumstances, it is little wonder that superior housing and a better environment remained out of the reach of the poor.

Unlike Glasgow, London and Liverpool, flats were uncommon in Birmingham. Indeed, there were only three small developments of them – at Milk Street, Palmer Street and Hospital Street. It was believed that Brummies were hostile to the idea of living in flats and this feeling had powerful support from the city's Medical Officer of Health, Dr Robertson. For many years he campaigned for the building of small houses to overcome the problems of homelessness and overcrowding in the city and in 1918 he advised strongly against the erection of flats. He was convinced that under no circumstances should they be contemplated as a substitute for back-to-backs, declaring that in time they would become even more 'unwholesome' than the dwellings they replaced. However, the realisation that the new council houses were not catering for the poor led some people to consider the building of flats. In 1923, H. Humphries, the City Engineer and Surveyor, made a report to the Public Works and Town Planning Committee which set out the predicament facing housing reformers in the city. Working-class people preferred houses and they were a desirable form of structure; yet, if a slum clearance scheme were begun, then the bulk of dishoused people would be unable to move to the suburbs because of distance, time and increased travelling costs. Given the paucity of vacant land in the central and middle wards that was suitable and available for housing, then the only way poor people could be rehoused locally was by the building of flats.

Osborne's fancy draper's, at 21 Hanley Street, Summer Lane neighbourhood, 1920s. (Sylvia Leigh).

In 1924, the Public Works and Town Planning Committee recognised that flats might have to be built if any slum clearance scheme was to be effective and responsive to the needs of the poor. The next year it pointed out to the council that the conditions of life in some parts of the city were no longer tolerable. Many back-to-backs were 100 years old, and were deteriorating rapidly, yet large numbers of their tenants could not afford the rents of new council houses. Cheaper accommodation was needed desperately and it was suggested that building costs – and so rents – could be lowered by constructing flats without baths. Accordingly, the council agreed to erect an experimental block of flats in a central district and to involve in the scheme the demolition of obstructive houses. The plan was abandoned because Birmingham's housing shortage was so acute that no dwellings, however undesirable, could afford to be lost. It was decided, therefore, to build on a former clay pit in Garrison Lane, near St Andrews. In 1927, 180 flats in three storey blocks were erected. They had a distinctive 'Dutch-style' look, but their tenants were not the poor who had originally been targeted for the new development. Overall, the residents were better-off working-class folk. This was because the government had insisted that baths be included in each flat and such a provision, as well as other modern amenities, led to weekly rents of between 8s 1d (40p) to 8s 10d (44p). In a mostly back-to-back neighbourhood, the flats were soon nicknamed 'The Mansions'.

The distinctive Dutch-style flats in Garrison Lane. Notice the tram lines.

Children playing tip cat in Studley Street, Sparkbrook, 1930s. Lenny Preston is in the foreground and Queen Street is in the background. (Lily Nead).

Birmingham councillors were not alone in recognising that since 1919 housing policies and programmes had done little to improve the conditions of the poor. The realisation of their ineffectiveness led Arthur Greenwood, Labour's Minister of Health, to introduce in 1930 a far-reaching and momentous act which lay the foundations of modern slum clearance. For the first time a government subsidy was provided specifically for slum clearance and it was related to the numbers of people displaced and rehoused. This was intended to prevent demolition without provision for rehousing, a practice common before 1914 and exemplified by the Corporation Street Improvement Scheme of 1875. It meant, too, that it was a subsidy on people rather than houses. This was a vitally important provision which made it easier for councils to rehouse large, poor families because the size of the subsidy increased with that of the family rehoused. In urban areas the grant was £2 5s (25p) per person for forty years, plus £1 5s (25p) on the same terms if the cost of acquiring sites was unusually high and flats, not houses, had to be built. Local authorities had to make a contribution of £3 15s (75p) per house or flat for the forty years and the level of rents were to be at their discretion. This allowed them to adopt rebate schemes, or differential renting, provided that the rents were what tenants could be reasonably expected to pay. Finally, local authorities had to submit slum-clearance plans with the aim of solving the problem within five years if possible.

Higher rents, a dearer standard of living, and costly travel had made new council houses unattractive to poorer people. More than that, in common with other authorities, Birmingham council had not intended them for the poor. It had adopted the principle of only letting houses to those who could afford the rent, in effect choosing its tenants according to the same criteria as private landlords. Under the scale used in 1926, a man with a wife and three children was accepted as a 'good tenant' of a three bedroom, non-parlour house only if he earned 70s (£3 50p) a week or more; whilst 80s (£4) a week was considered the minimum wage necessary for a 'good tenant' of a three-bedroom parlour home. This was at a time when a wage of 50s (£2 50p) a week was regarded as 'good' by many working-class people. Greenwood's Act, then, at last held out the prospect of the provision of decent houses at a rental low enough for poor families. This was recognised in Birmingham and once again a Conservative led council adopted enthusiastically an important piece of social legislation passed by a Labour government. It informed the Ministry of Health that it intended to build 30,000 houses over the next five years – 23,000 of them under Wheatley's Act, and 7,000 as part of a plan of slum clearance programme.

Brew'us in Court Number 10, back of 42-45 Cecil Street, Summer Lane neighbourhood, close to the 'White Swan on the corner of Hanley Street, 1935. (Sylvia Leigh). Mrs G.W. Stevens lived nearby in Unett Street where the rent of their back-to-back house was 6s (30p) a week: 'One living room, one bedroom, one attic and a pantry. Gas mantle light. No running water. Coal fire. Black grate. My mother polished it with black lead till it shone.'

By 1930 urgent attention was needed to slum clearance and the housing problems of the poor. Although 30,000 corporation dwellings had been built since 1919, this large figure did not even meet the requirements of the city, for by 30 June 1930 there were 31,732 applicants still waiting to be given a municipal house. Consequently, overcrowding had increased – with the proportion of houses occupied by two or more families rising from 19% in 1914 to 34% in 1925. The council's ambitious housing programme in response to Greenwood's Act was essential, but it was faced by severe difficulties. Foremost was the growing shortage of land for development, a problem most pressing in the central wards where new housing was needed desperately. The building of the planned minimum of 5,000 new houses annually would require 400 acres and that was without the needs of private development and slum clearance. In its quest for viable options for its housing programme the council sent a deputation to Germany, Czechoslovakia and Austria to inquire into the provision of flats for working-class people. It visited Hamburg, Berlin, Prague, Vienna, Munich, Frankfurt and Cologne, and whilst its report remained in favour of self-contained houses, it accepted that in certain circumstances flats would be a necessary response to the housing problem.

The rear of numbers 1-7, Prince's Row, off Howe Street in the Cardigan Street neighbourhood 1964. Photographs such as these emphasise how long-drawn out was the attack on slum housing. (Johnny Landon). In 1932 Councillor Alderson declared that 'the main object should now be to build cheaper houses for the poor people who so far have not had the chance of a house. There is a genuine desire in the City Council to fulfil this obligation, and also at the same time to provide better houses for those compelled to live in the slums.' (Social Questions, 1934). The fact that houses like these in Prince's Row still had tenants in the mid-1960s indicates the dashing of the hopes of Councillor Alderson and others.

The council deputation felt that certain amenities were essential if flats were to be provided satisfactorily, but it was believed that this aim could be achieved only if the 'colony' was a large one of 500 to 1,000 dwellings. A maximum height of four storeys was preferred, whilst the blocks ought to be laid out on town planning lines, so permitting the full enjoyment of sunshine and fresh air. Finally, the deputation recommended that up to 1,000 flats should be included in the five year programme for slum housing. Not until 1932 was any progress made in the matter. Following an article in the *Evening Despatch* it was agreed to build 175, two storey maisonettes in Great Brook Street, Ashted on the site of a former cavalry barracks. All had a large living room, scullery and bathroom, two or three bedrooms, and they were divided in to six sections – each surrounding an asphalt area for playing and drying. Until this development, a mere 355 new dwellings had been built in the central wards since 1918. With regard to housing, time had seemed to stand still. Whilst new houses with modern amenities were erected in the suburbs, the residents of increasingly decayed back-to-backs had to be content with Nettlefold's turn-of-the century policy of patching and improvement. The Ashcroft Estate was the first housing development in Birmingham brought in specifically as part of a substantial slum clearance programme, but it was too small to improve the lives of all but a tiny minority of the poor.

The first house to be occupied on the Ashcroft Estate, 18 August 1933. This estate in Vauxhall was opened officially on 23 October 1934 by Edward, Prince of Wales.

The Ashcroft Estate had not been intended as the first development of flats in Birmingham. Following the deputation's report, a recommendation was made in 1931 that a block of flats be erected on a five acre site close to the city centre. It was bounded by Angelina, Dymoke, Leopold and Vaughton Streets and was crossed by Emily Street. A discussion about the type of dwelling to be built there was won by those favouring maisonettes, but the city's overall housing programme was threatened by a shortage of bricklayers and plasterers and this plan was abandoned. Accordingly, the Emily Street area was chosen as the site of an experimental block of concrete flats which provided an alternative to traditional brick-constructed homes. In January 1934 the council declared the site a clearance area and it was estimated that 257 dwellings would be required to rehouse the 1,283 people displaced by the scheme. In the event, by 1939, 267 flats with balconies had been built. They varied from one to three bedrooms, were erected in four-storey blocks, and had refuse disposal chutes placed opposite all staircases. Drying rooms were provided on each floor and there were plans for playgrounds, gardens with seats, and a bowling green. Birmingham's final development of flats before 1939 was at Kingston Road, Bordesley, where the existing property was cleared and ninety eight, two and three bedroom maisonettes were built in 1937. They were erected in twenty-five blocks and each had a sun balcony.

The Emily Street flats the day before they were opened by the Queen on 2 March 1939.

The council's 1930 housing programme had planned for 7,000 dwellings as part of a slum clearance scheme over the next five years. Flats and maisonettes built at Emily Street, Great Brook Street and Kingston Road did not even approach that target. The council had failed to achieve its goal and to provide effectively and substantially for the housing needs of the city's poor. Its failure was not due to any insensitivity to the plight of poor people nor to a lack of desire to help them. Rather, the council's enterprising programme had foundered on the rock of the economic crisis on to which the nation had crashed in 1931. In an atmosphere of gloom and pessimism, and with a depression sweeping the country, high-spending housing schemes were discarded. Everywhere, retrenchment and cutting back were triumphant. Birmingham was no different and the supporters of economy held sway over a small minority of councillors from all parties who strove to maintain an active housing policy. Consequently, the city's housing scheme was cut and its register for municipal houses slashed. Council house-building slumped, but private building boomed. Its construction rate trebled between 1930 and 1935, increasing phenomenally from one quarter of the council's output to six times it. Home ownership was boosted by falling construction costs, low interest rates, the approval of 90% advances to purchasers instead of 70%, and a general rise in real wages for those in work. Soon, private homes were as familiar as municipal houses in the outer ring, but their appearance – welcome as it was – did little to solve Birmingham's housing problem.

Celebrations for the silver jubilee of King George V at Cranbourne Road Infants School, Kingstanding. (Terry A. V. Thomas).

As early as 1840, a House of Commons Select Committee had condemned back-to-backs as unsuitable for people to live in. Nearly 100 years later, poverty still forced tens of thousands of Brummies to rent these life-destroying houses. National and local government had failed to provide an alternative of cheaply-rented but good quality accommodation. Modern homes fitted with up-to-date conveniences were erected in the suburbs, but in the central wards the twentieth century was held at bay. Without slum clearance and rebuilding, the council's only response to the problems of bad housing remained the Edwardian policy of slum patching. In 1925 a group of Birmingham citizens realised that for the foreseeable future many people would remain living in dilapidated homes. Consequently, they formed the Birmingham Copec House Improvement Society with the aim of buying slum properties and putting them in as good repair as possible. The policy began in 1926 when nineteen back-to-backs in Pope Street were re-roofed, re-plastered, and re-decorated; given new floors, grates, and repaired staircases; and installed with gas and a cold water supply. Copec's good work continued elsewhere, but together with the council's action of property improvement it barely stemmed the tide of bad housing. Indeed, many houses were beyond repair. Between 1930 and 1939, 8,000 dwellings were declared unfit and most were demolished. As had happened at the turn of the century, slum clearance without re-building could only lead to overcrowding.

Councillor Mrs E.L. Hobson viewing the poor state of the small scullery of Mrs F. Jones at 5 back of 101, Hingeston Street, Brookfields, 28 April 1966. Tens of thousands of women had struggled in conditions like these from the nineteenth century onwards. Notice the crock sink and the chip pan and flat iron on the shelves. (Birmingham Evening Mail*).*

Overcrowding was a national problem and in 1935 a housing act was passed which aimed at its eradication. It set a standard of accommodation and required local authorities to ascertain overcrowding in their areas and to submit a report and plans for its abatement. Crucially, provision was made for redeveloping districts where there were 50 or more working-class houses. If a third of them were overcrowded or unfit for habitation, then the locality could be declared a redevelopment area subject to a redevelopment plan. Property could be reconditioned and the act allowed for government subsidies towards the erection of flats on expensive sites which were purchased – either to relieve overcrowding or for a redevelopment scheme. The act revived municipal house-building in Birmingham and between the end of 1935 and 1938, 7,931 corporation houses were built as opposed to 3,851 in the previous three years. The necessity of new homes was indicated by the 1936 council report into overcrowding. It estimated that if living rooms were excluded as sleeping accommodation, then 13.5% of families were overcrowded. Moreover, there remained 38,773 back-to-backs in Birmingham; 51,794 houses without separate toilets; and despite attempts to lay on water supplies to each dwelling, 13,650 still depended on a communal tap. Over, 3,500 new houses were required to deal with statutory overcrowding, and authority was given to provide for between 1,000 and 1,500 four-bedroom homes as the first step in this programme.

Court 36 in Woodcock Street, near Gosta Green, 1930s. This shows the yard looking up towards the entrance at which the mother, child and elderly lady were photographed on p.46. In 1938 the Estates Committee summarised Birmingham's housing requirements for the next six years: for normal needs, 10,038 houses; for slum clearance, 23,400; and for overcrowding, 3,525. This gave a total of 36,962. The coming of war ensured these figures would never be met.

It would have been better if more dwellings had been built during the worst years of the depression when construction costs had been low and unemployment in the building trade could have been alleviated. Still, the commitment to providing new homes was welcomed by many – whatever their regrets about past policy. Yet over the intervening years a drastic shortage of houses had accumulated, resulting in too few dwellings to meet the combined needs of slum clearance, overcrowding and normal building. Even with a renewed commitment to municipal house construction, the Estates Department indicated that only 2,200 dwellings would be completed in 1936 because of too few bricklayers and plasterers. Concerned over the housing shortage, the council instructed the Estates and Public Health Committees (Housing Conference) to prepare a housing programme for a fixed period of years. Following this, the Public Works Committee was to make proposals for construction. In 1938 the magnitude of the undertaking faced by the city became apparent when the Housing Conference presented its report which was adopted by the council. Over the next six years a total of nearly 37,000 new dwellings were required to meet the city's needs. This figure was beyond the ability of the city to cope with, and it agreed that 25,000 dwellings were to be provided over the next five years at an annual rate of 5,000. A realistic hope was at last offered for tenants of unhealthy property, as slum clearance and overcrowding were to account for 4,000 of this yearly figure.

A rare shot above ground and showing the overcrowding of space in a working-class neighbourhood, in this case King Edward's Road, Ladywood, 20 January 1950.

Birmingham's post-war redevelopment was influenced heavily by three significant pre-war events: the 1935 Housing Act; the city's 1938 Housing Conference Report; and the appointment of Herbert Manzoni as City Engineer and Surveyor in 1935. His influence on the appearance of Birmingham was immense and it owed much to his astute use of both national and local legislation. Taking advantage of the redevelopment provisions of the 1935 Act, he prepared a plan for 267 acres of Duddeston, Ashted and Nechells. In December 1937 the scheme was approved by the council and the district was declared a redevelopment area. The plan was acknowledged as unprecedented both in its scope as a rehousing scheme and in its cost – the great sum of £6,000,000. It also placed Birmingham in the national limelight as this was by far the most extensive redevelopment project yet in England. Existing residential properties in the area were to be cleared and unlike the former layout there was to be a clear separation between residential and industrial zones and the provision of open spaces. So influential was this scheme that by 1941 the Public Works Department was drawing up plans for another three redevelopment areas in the Gooch Street, Summer Lane and Ladywood districts. The scene was set for the transformation of the run-down central wards of Birmingham.

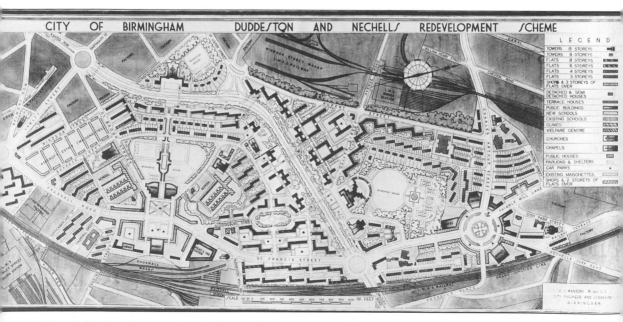

Plan indicating the separation of redeveloped Duddeston and Nechells into zones for houses, factories and open spaces. In 1955 in the Journal of the Town Planning Institute, *Herbert Manzoni, the City Engineer and Surveyor explained his belief that 'to bring back an obsolete district to a high standard ... can only be achieved if the whole layout is changed with the proper zoning, and all the amenities of a new and up-to-date development; to rebuild a few groups of houses in an already dingy setting will never do this – the whole area must be new and it must look completely different.*

Manzoni's plan assumed that only about 70% of cleared residential properties would be replaced on any one site. Consequently, the remaining 30% of the population would have to be rehoused elsewhere in the city. This necessity would cause problems given the increasing shortage of building land in Birmingham. The solution relied on the recommendations of the 1938 Housing Conference Report which had altered radically the city's housing policy. Apart from the four experiments in providing flats at Garrison Lane, Great Brook Street, Emily Street, and Kingston Road, the council had insisted on building houses for working-class people. The housing shortage and the rapid decline in land available for development, led the conference to recommend that in future flats had to be an integral part of the city's building programme. Of the 25,000 dwellings which were to be built over the next five years, 15,000 were to be flats or maisonettes. As far as was practicable, they were to be constructed on internal sites, whilst the 10,000 houses of the programme were to be erected on land on the city's outskirts already purchased for rehousing purposes. Manzoni's predecessor as City Engineer and Surveyor was Herbert Humphries and although he had accepted the need of building some flats to help in slum clearance he did not see them as a large part of the solution to the housing problem. Manzoni did, and in his powerful position he was able to implement the change in the council's policy. The era of redevelopment and high rise flats was at hand, although it was to be postponed for ten years by the Second World War.

A woman looks out of the windowless brew'us on to a yard where blue bricks only form a footpath in front of the houses, 1930s. Notice the little cart and the sacks of coal in front of the house in the doorway of which are standing two young children.

Chapter 3:

The Attack on the Slums

In August 1940 a lone German raider bombed Erdington, signalling the start of the Blitz on Birmingham. For the rest of that year and in to 1942, the Luftwaffe pounded the city in an attempt to destroy factories as well as the determination of Brummies to defeat Hitler. After London and along with Liverpool, Birmingham was the most-heavily bombed British city. Tragedies were numerous, especially in the poorer, central districts which bore the brunt of the Nazis' fury. One of the worst disasters of the war occurred on 25 October 1940 when a single bomb killed nineteen people at the Carlton Picture House in Sparkbrook; and on 19 November 1940, 350 bombers pulverised city, killing about 400 people, including nearly fifty munitions workers at the BSA in Small Heath. Despite the ferocity of the attacks, Brummies remained resolute; as one air-raid victim put it, 'Though our houses are down, our spirits are up'. Still, the Blitz took a terrible toll of life and health: 2,241 Brummies were killed, 3,010 were injured seriously, and 3,682 were hurt slightly. The face of the city, too, was affected badly by the raids, as familiar landmarks like the Market Hall, the Empire Music Hall and the Prince of Wales Theatre were burned out and destroyed.

Damaged houses and a bomb crater in Vincent Street, Balsall Heath, October 1940. In her book My Mother's Story *(1986), Wyn Heywood told of the effects of the terrible bombing attacks on this area and nearby Highgate in the following month: 'I did, however, go to my brother's funeral, and it was a scene I can still see now. The whole of Bishop Street and Gooch Street were lined with people crying. Almost every person there had suffered loss through the raids and that was why it was so crowded and deeply touching.'*

During the 'phoney war' period of 1939, large numbers of Brummie children were evacuated to places less likely to be bombed. However, the delayed start to the Luftwaffe's attacks lulled people into a false sense of security, and many evacuees returned to the city just before the Blitz began. Once it started the Nazi's targeted Birmingham's poorer neighbourhoods, where houses mingled with factories turned over to the war effort. Despite the danger there was no mass flight to the safer suburbs. Tenaciously, working-class families defied Hitler's wrath, staying in tumble-down back-to-backs which they would have been glad to leave peacefully but not through coercion. Still, the bombings destroyed houses, and altogether 103,919 were obliterated or damaged. Of these, 4,601 were destroyed totally or were blown up so badly that demolition was necessary; 13,311 were bombed so seriously that their tenants had to be evacuated; and a further 12,126 were damaged severely but remained useable. Obviously, house-building had ceased when the war began, but the council strove to provide accommodation for those made homeless. Five hundred and seventeen individual houses were converted in to 1,057 flatlets; 100 large dwellings became hostels for the short-term accommodation of bombed-out families; and another 801 badly-damaged houses were repaired and re-tenanted. More significantly, councillors and planners had begun to pay attention to the housing needs of the city once the war was over.

A depot for the repair and maintenance of council houses in College Road, Perry Common. Many children were evacuated from Birmingham in order to keep them away from bombing raids. Most were sent away during the phoney war period of late 1939 and returned home before the Blitz began in the autumn of 1940. One person who was not evacuated was Ron Smith: 'To quote "Our Mom's" actual words, she said, "Yo' ain't guin' now'ere, non' on ya' ain't, yome stoppin' 'ere with ya' fertha an' me, weem all gunna stop tergetha, that's w'at weem gunna do". This is exactly what we did . . .' (Ron Smith, Guest Street, Hockley, A Paddle in Hockley Brook, nd).

With the outbreak of war, the Ministry of Health ordered slum clearance and construction to cease, although Birmingham continued to buy building land. Effectively, the process of redevelopment became dormant, but councillors were determined that it should not be aborted. In 1942, under the impetus of Lord Mayor Norman Tiptaft, the council established a Reconstruction Committee to co-ordinate plans to revitalise Birmingham after the war. Its grandiose ideas led to its demise in 1944, but fortunately many of its objectives were dealt with by the Public Works Committee which was committed to the task of preparing for peace time. It set up several panels to consider and advise on problems which would need urgent attention after the war. Their members included representatives from commerce, industry and the professions as well as councillors. One panel concentrated on the obstacles besetting redevelopment and it instructed surveys to be drawn up of all the obsolete property in the city. Its work led to the decision to schedule for redevelopment the Bath Row, Gooch Street, Ladywood and Summer Lane areas, whilst further progress was made in 1943 when the council approved the definitive scheme for Duddeston and Nechells. Still, planners were aware acutely of the difficulty of turning ideas in to reality. Birmingham's proposals came under the 1935 Housing Act which did not really provide for schemes of this magnitude. If massive redevelopment was to happen, then new laws were needed speedily.

Bomb damage in Bridge Street West, Hockley, 30 July 1942. (Birmingham Library Services). The official start of the post-war housing programme came in April 1945. Between then and 1947, the Housing Department was only able to allocate an average of thirty-nine dwellings a week, when 500 were needed. One of the problems faced by the council was that 'additional to that which faced most of the big cities' there was an shortage of skilled trades in the building industry owing to the attraction of factory work. This led to an invitation to non-traditional, or new tradition builders to the city. (A. G. Sheppard Fidler, City Architect, The Builder, 1957)

During June 1943, the Ministry of Town and Country Planning set up an Advisory Panel on Redevelopment of City Centres. It sat until August 1944 and its task was to consider the best way to administer the rehabilitation of bomb-damaged towns once the war was over. Visits were made to most of the areas harmed by the Blitz, and the panel were affected deeply by the problems of cities like Coventry and Plymouth whose centres had been destroyed completely in a few nights' sustained bombing. By contrast, the attacks on Birmingham had been more drawn out and they had damaged a wider area. Consequently, its inner localities had not been 'coventried' and it would not have benefited from the panel's initial recommendations for legislation. However, one of its members was Herbert Manzoni, Birmingham's' highly-respected city engineer. He persuaded his fellow representatives that the problems of redeveloping obsolete districts were similar to those of rehabilitating war-damaged areas, indeed probably they were more extensive. Consequently, the Ministry accepted the panel's recommendations, passing the Town Planning Act of 1944. Also known as the Blitz and Blight Act, it gave local authorities sweeping powers of acquisition for blitzed and obsolete areas and it included provisions for financial aid from the government. In Manzoni's words, 'the city was waiting just for this very act'.

Mick Guilfoyle, his aunt Edna Dodd and cousin Fred Dodd outside one of the Nissen Huts which had been set up for the Army Camp on Billesley Common during the Second World War, about 1946. Mick Guilfoyle recalled that when peace came, 'overcrowded families moved into these Nissen Huts, becoming known then as "the squatters" – rough and ready families but with a special friendship'. (Mick Guilfoyle).

Mrs Ethel Birkett of Eyre Street, Spring Hill was woken up in the night by one of her eight children because he could see light coming through his bedroom, 8 June 1966. She had lived in the house for twenty-four years and for the previous seventeen had been trying for another house, 'but it seems hopeless'. She lived in the last part of the road which had not been pulled down and had regularly complained about holes in the bedroom wall, unsafe floors and the dust nuisance whilst the house next door was demolished. After this incident, Mrs Birkett was informed she would not be in the house much longer and soon would be made an offer for a four-bedroom house. (Birmingham Evening Mail).

Alongside its plan for redevelopment, the council paid serious attention to the city's housing problem. This was a matter of urgency given the lack of construction since 1939 and the influx of war workers to Birmingham, whilst it was to be exacerbated after 1945 by a rise in the city's birth rate. In 1944, the Public Works Committee announced its first hesitant yet ambitious proposals for a post-war housing policy. Ten thousand dwellings would be required to meet the housing deficiency which existed in 1939; a further 10,000 were needed to replace homes destroyed or made uninhabitable by the bombing; 50,000 houses would have to be provided as part of a slum clearance programme; and 30,000 dwellings had to be built before December 1953 to cater for fifteen years' normal housing demands from December 1938. It was hoped that private builders would erect two-thirds of this latter figure, allowing the council to concentrate on tackling the housing deficiency and homelessness caused by the war. As a result, the corporation proposed to build 30,000 high standard houses in the shortest possible time, aiming at providing 5,000 of them in the first year of the programme. It was hoped that a concerted three-year attack on this part of the housing problem would then allow a huge transfer of resources to slum clearance and redevelopment. This aspect of the council's policy was acknowledged to be a much thornier difficulty which would take between twenty and thirty years to complete.

Birmingham's proposals for post-war reconstruction were far-sighted and adventurous and the city approached the coming of peace with an air of optimism. Its planning proceeded at three levels: the global, intermediate and micro. Global policy dealt with the overall, city-wide strategy for the housing programme, redevelopment and slum clearance, whilst at an intermediate layer plans were drawn up for the shape and nature of specific areas. Significantly, the design of future council estates was affected by criticisms of those built between the wars. Rightly, these had been praised for an environment superior to that of the drab central wards, but their residents had condemned their layouts as hindering neighbourliness and stifling the emergence of small, localised communities. Therefore it was decided to adopt a concept of planning based on the neighbourhood unit of the New York Regional Plan, 1928. Wherever possible, new council estates were to be considered as self-contained units of about 10,000 people. These neighbourhoods would be provided with their own shops and special buildings such as schools, community halls, branch libraries and clinics, whilst the housing was to be of all types and sizes. Ideally, they would also be economic entities so that residents could find work near to their homes and thus increase the social cohesion of the districts. This arrangement was introduced first at five large outer-city estates at Sheldon, Quinton, Harborne and Washwood Heath, and then extended to the redevelopment areas. It was not easy to implement the concept, but its acceptance did indicate some willingness to listen to tenants.

*Studying a model of what the Gooch Street and Bath Row neighbourhoods would look like after redevelopment are members of Birmingham's Redevelopment sub-Committee. Left to right are: Sir Herbert Manzoni, regarded by many as the driving force behind the emergence of a new Birmingham after the Second World War; Alderman G. Griffith; Alderman Frank Price, a leading Labour politician; and Councillor A. E. Benton. (*The New Birmingham, *no date, thanks to Mrs B. Spurrier).*

The intermediate planning level was complemented by a micro strategy which attended to the design of houses and here again the influence of working-class people was felt. One of the city's war-time advisory committees focused on possible designs for new council houses and on the domestic equipment that they would need to be provided with. It was recognised that those who knew most about this subject were the people who lived in corporation dwellings and so six Brummie housewives, all council tenants, were appointed to the committee. Its inquiries were supplemented by research which involved the construction of two model kitchens. The result of these detailed investigations was unequivocal. Post-war houses had to be roomier than those built in the inter-war years and they had to be provided with better facilities. A standard house would remain three bedroom, but its total area would increase from 760 square feet to 870. It would have a through hall and large living room downstairs; a bathroom and separate water closet upstairs; and at the back, a small wash-house, water closet and covered space for the dustbin. The most significant improvements were associated with the kitchen. This would be provided with built-in cupboards, a drying room, a hatch connecting it to the living room, two draining boards, a fitted table, a large cupboard for kitchen utensils, larder, coalhouse and delivery hatch.

Children crossing the new dual carriageway, Nechells Parkway, set to link Great Lister Street in the fore-ground with Ashted Row. The new high-rise flats on the right overlook Victorian housing on the left. (Birmingham Evening Mail*).*

In 1941, the Bournville Village Trust had brought out a thoughtful study on housing and town planning called *When We Build Again*. Its authors had identified reconstruction as the most important national initiative after the war effort. People seemed animated by a desire to avoid the mistakes and pitfalls which had plagued reformers after 1919. No matter how appealing, a slogan such as Homes Fit for Heroes could not build houses nor create a better world. As the Bournville Village Trust investigation indicated, if there was to be progress then central direction and inspiration were essential. No longer could Birmingham stand alone, interpreting national legislation in its own adventurous and semi-independent way for the benefit of its citizens. It could still be forward thinking, as indicated by its redevelopment schemes or its adoption of the neighbourhood unit strategy, also referred to in Abercrombie's Greater London Plan, 1944. But schemes and strategies could be implemented and made effective only with the deep involvement of central government. Thus, Birmingham's thoughtful inquiries in to the design of post-war houses were over-shadowed by the contemporary Dudley Report (1944). This, too, recognised that the living space of inter-war council houses was cramped and it also acknowledged the importance of kitchens and the need to improve facilities within new dwellings. But Birmingham's innovative research and recommendations never received the national acknowledgement they deserved precisely because they reflected national trends. Now, Birmingham was tied clearly to national policy.

A mother in Heaton Street, Hockley striving to stay clean as had so many mothers before her, 1950s. Notice the terry nappies on the line and the tin bath hanging on the wall. (Birmingham Evening Mail) Mrs Cartmell, who lived nearby in New Spring Street, Brookfields, remembered the attic in a similar house 'which was lit by a paraffin lamp, and the bathroom and living room were lit by gas mantle jet. I had to pass houses that were bombed during the war. Mom had to get up early to get the copper going with the old peelings and slack we riddled out of the coal. We had an old brown crock sink, a tin bath on the cellar head for our Friday night bath.'

With the arrival of peace in 1945, Birmingham seemed well prepared to tackle its housing problem once and for all. In most respects it was in a more advantageous position than other local authorities. It had a coherent housing programme, considered housing strategies and five defined redevelopment areas. These covered nearly 1,400 acres, of which almost 1,000 were obsolete property. All had been surveyed; draft zoning and tentative layouts had been made; the city council had given its approval of the schemes; and in February 1946 it made the Compulsory Purchase Order necessary to allow it to take over property in the areas. Thus, Birmingham was committed to the purchase of about 30,000 sub-standard dwellings, their clearance and the building of new towns on their site. Moreover, it was determined to remedy the housing deficiency by a swift building campaign so that full attention could be given to redevelopment. In this wish it was frustrated, although the newly-elected Labour government wanted to help and had set a national target of building 240,000 houses per year. In 1946 it passed a Housing Act which provided a Treasury subsidy of £16 10s (50p) per new house for sixty years, so long as the local authority gave a grant of £5 10s (50p). However, as after 1919, aspirations were confounded by pitiless economic reality. The goodwill of the government was negated by insufficient resources which were stretched to breaking point by the competing claims of industrial reconstruction, nationalisation and the welfare state programmes.

Women in Cook Street, Nechells with a petition complaining about their housing conditions, 2 July 1968. On the left is Mrs M. E. Oldacres followed by Mrs Levy (at the back), Mrs Blakemoor, Mrs Lamb, Mrs Keane, Mrs Devlin and Mrs Bell. (Birmingham Evening Mail). *Mrs Irene Foster was not rehoused from 3, back of 33, New Street, Aston until 1969: 'the toilet was at the top of the yard, there were two but one never worked for years. It was shared by the top two families, the other six families shared the two toilets in the yard below. They were all wood with just a toilet bowl in the centre, the handle to flush was usually string.'*

Not until the summer of 1945 was the government able to authorise a start to building, and even then Birmingham's housing programme was threatened by severe shortages of labour and materials. The council had recognised this likelihood in 1944, anticipating that it would have to adopt unusual construction methods if it were to achieve its target of erecting 5,000 houses in the first year after the war. The desperate scarcity of skilled labour and of traditional building materials such as brick could be overcome only if houses were built non-traditionally. Birmingham was well-prepared for this eventuality. Apart from Coventry, it was the only council to have experimented with building types during the war, erecting two trial steel-framed houses at Alum Rock. Their interiors were permanent and included a considerable measure of prefabrication, whilst their exteriors were clothed with temporary materials of a good quality and which could be replaced later by brick-work and tile without the moving out of the tenants. However, by mid 1945 support had swung away from them, although 500 were put up in Sheldon in 1949 after an offer from the British Iron and Steel Corporation. Two other experimental houses were constructed. This time it was with the concrete system developed by the local firm Bryant's, but they proved too costly to be of use to the council.

Spraying the pre-cast concrete components of the factory made houses at the Housing Development Industries factory in Stratford, 24 June 1964. These units were to be used for building houses in Shard End. (Birmingham Evening Mail).

Churchill's war-time government, too, had recognised the need of erecting non-traditional houses. In 1944 it announced plans to mass produce prefabricated dwellings which could be assembled on site by unskilled labour. At first, Birmingham council was opposed to accepting any prefabs as it believed them to be an inferior form of accommodation. However, by the end of 1944 the dearth of normal building resources made this position untenable. Reluctantly, the council agreed to take 2,500 prefabs as soon as they were available. These were to be erected on council owned sites; whilst another 2,000 were to be put up on private plots. Wherever possible, they were to be placed on the street frontages of parks or open spaces but not on sites identified for permanent houses. These provisos, as well as a shortage of materials, meant that in 1945 only 325 temporary houses were finished. The following year matters improved with the completion of another 1,475 prefabs. Altogether 4,625 of these dwellings were put up, including 552 made in America and obtained under lease-lend. Though factory made, they boasted two bedrooms, a fitted kitchen, toilet and bathroom and were far better than homelessness. As predicted by Manzoni and Alderman Tiptaft, many of these temporary buildings became permanent. Some were removed in 1955-56 at the end of their intended ten year life, but in 1972 there remained 1,800 of them and seventeen are tenanted still on the Wake Green Road, Moseley. Now rewired insulated and modernised, these prefabs are now listed buildings.

Flats at Tile Cross, with prefabs in the foreground, 21 November 1954. (Birmingham Evening Mail). In 1994, Birmingham's last prefabs on the Wake Green Road, Moseley became listed as buildings of historical and architectural importance. Tom and Pat Attenberrow have lived there since October 1968, attracted by the coal-fired living room, kitchen, two bedrooms, bathroom, toilet and garden. In 1977, when the council announced proposals for demolition, the Attenberrows joined with their neighbours and local historians to fight the plans.

By 1946 prefabs were becoming familiar features in Birmingham, but the rate of construction of permanent houses was most unsatisfactory. A meagre six had been finished in 1945, with a scanty 413 the following year, and a slightly better figure of 826 in 1947. The total inadequacy of this number was emphasised when it was revealed that in the same year there were over 50,000 applicants on the city's housing register. Homelessness in Birmingham and elsewhere appeared to be an unmanageable problem. True, the major blame was a national scarcity of building materials and labour, but the council must have regretted its hasty decision not to proceed with erecting steel-framed dwellings. The dream of post-war reconstruction had become a nightmare which daily was worsening. By June 1948 the waiting list for homes had swollen to nearly 65,000 names, and the council tried desperately to stem its further increase. Exchanges and relets were increased, house-building was rationalised, and in 1949 changes were made to the points system. This had been established in 1945 to ensure a fair allocation of dwellings to applicants on the housing register, but the city's crisis of homelessness led to the introduction of a five-year residential qualification and an emphasis on housing special cases. These strategies reduced the waiting list to 50,000 names, but the building rate remained low and without a drastic increase there seemed little prospect of a further fall in homelessness.

Mrs Shirley Jones 'lives, cooks, washes and tries to amuse four young children in this room', 11 September 1969. In the yard outside, sewers and cisterns overflowed, whilst the cellar of the house was waterlogged and infested by rats. (Birmingham Evening Mail*). In 1960 Bevan Laing moved into the attic high 1 back of 101, Clarke Street, Ladywood: 'There was just enough room in the kitchen for the small white sink and small cooker . . . above the sink there was a small cupboard which was too small to hold the required saucepans and crockery of an average family. There was a wall cupboard in the downstairs room, but as at all times it was crawling with beetles we were unable to use it . . . when it rained for some time the cellar was like a lake.'*

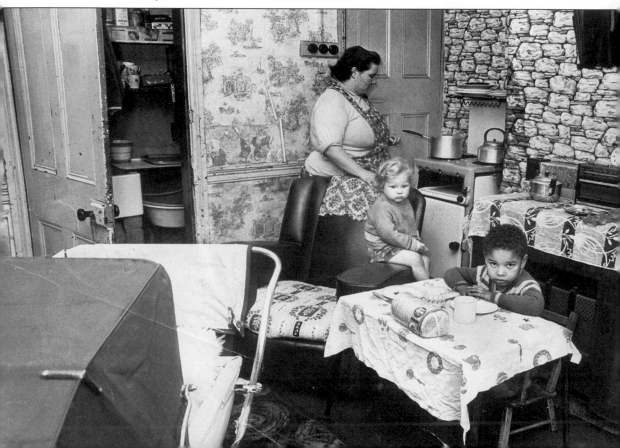

Nationally, building rates fell short of the Labour government's target of 240,000 houses a year, but Birmingham's progress was worse than most local authorities. During the year ending March 1949, it erected just 1.39 municipal dwellings per thousand people, compared to a national average of 3.72. Indeed, for the year ending June 1949 its production of new permanent dwellings was less than half that achieved by other large cities in England and Wales. This situation was intolerable and after the local elections of 1949 the council set up a Standing Joint Housing Committee to investigate the city's tardy building rate. It was a cross-party group comprised of councillors from various committees concerned with housing. Since 1945 this issue had dominated local politics in Birmingham. Certainly there were differences between the Conservatives, who advocated a greater reliance on private enterprise to solve the housing problem, and Labour, who opposed the erection of experimental houses. Still, Birmingham politics was not as confrontationist as elsewhere, indeed the Conservatives had claimed to be the most 'Socialist' of Conservative-controlled municipalities before 1939. Both parties were determined to eradicate the slums, to build as many municipal house s as possible, and to create a better environment for Brummies. Despite their political disagreements, there was a fundamental and much-needed consensus over housing policy.

Clara Bartholomew with a neighbour's children in Barr Street, Hockley, late 1940s. (Mrs Beryl Brooks). In 1947 a report in the Birmingham Evening Despatch *stated that 'Birmingham's housing queue is still growing at the rate of 350 a week. On 9 August there were 58,384 names on the register ... On some days 1,000 people wanting homes plead their case at the Estates Department. Its postbag averages 500 letters a day.'*

The Joint Housing Conference blamed Birmingham's inferior rate of construction on the city's acute labour shortage and its wastage of the building workers available. To counter these worries it proposed that more non-traditional houses should be built. The Public Works Committee accepted this, planning to include 2,000 of them in its 1950 building programme. Moreover, it decided to abandon local construction firms which had fallen behind with their municipal contracts. Instead it would invite to Birmingham several large building concerns which were capable of erecting non-traditional dwellings on a large scale. At the same time, the council argued that the Ministry of Health had to loosen its tight control over local-authority building so that it could plan ahead and erect more houses. This was done. Such beneficial changes in local and central government policy meant that the city's building rate increased from 1,227 dwellings in 1949 to a peak of 4,744 by 1952, by which year the housing register had fallen to 43,000 applicants. Vitally, both Conservative and Labour representatives had supported most of the recommendations made by the Joint Housing Committee. This harmony was crucial for the future well-being of the city. It meant that housing policy in Birmingham would remain consistent whatever political party was in control, allowing Brummies to benefit from long-term planning.

A living room in a council house, late 1950s. This shows how even modern accommodation could be cramped if the family were large.

In 1947 the Minister of Health confirmed Birmingham's Compulsory Purchase Order on its redevelopment areas. The scene was set for slum clearance and rehousing on a scale never before witnessed in the city, and there was little doubt that it was needed desperately. Soon after the war the council had ordered a comprehensive housing survey of Birmingham and its results made depressing reading. Since 1936, demolitions and bombing had reduced the number of back-to-backs by nearly 10,000, but still over 29,000 were left – almost 60% of them in the redevelopment areas. There lingered around 6,500 dwellings without a separate water supply, and again 60% were in Birmingham's five blighted districts. Another 35,000 houses still had shared toilets, 81,500 had no bath, and appallingly, there remained 417 dwellings with no gas or electricity. Overall there were over 50,000 unfit houses in the city. This was one in six if all dwellings, a proportion exceeded nationally only in Liverpool and Manchester. These statistics could give only a vague impression of the distressing conditions under which tens of thousands of Brummies lived. Valiantly they defied tremendous odds, striving to lead decent lives in the most inhospitable environment. After such shocking revelations, Manzoni hoped that the council would transfer its resources to slum clearance. But it was preoccupied with the grave problem of the burgeoning housing register and redevelopment was put on hold.

Mrs June Batchelor of 3 back of 32, Upper Thomas Street, Aston, living in the only one of six houses still occupied in her yard. Still waiting to be rehoused, she told reporters, 'I am terrified each night', 15 March 1967. (Birmingham Evening Mail).

The 1947 Housing Survey Report led the Estates Committee to allocate one-quarter of all new dwellings to slum clearance. However, the current rate of building in the city was too low to allow a start to this operation and the council had to accept that large numbers of people would have to live in unacceptable accommodation for some years to come. In these circumstances it was imperative that their environment should be improved as much as possible, without too great an expenditure on houses with a low life expenditure. Therefore, the council embarked on a short-term policy of reconditioning slum property. 'Soling and heeling', as it was now called, had long been established as a central feature of Birmingham's housing programme. The Corporation Street Improvement Scheme (1875) had been the city's first involvement in redevelopment, and although it did not rehouse those made homeless under its operations it did improve 1,000 dwellings. Under the prodding of Councillors Cook and Nettlefold, reconditioning of this kind became the key element of the city's assault on the housing problem before 1914. Moreover, in the absence of redevelopment in the inter-war years, it remained a crucial strategy within the central wards, alongside the demolition of insanitary property. Slum patching it may have been, but to those who dwelt in dilapidated back-to-backs any improvement in the standard of their homes was welcome.

*Soled and heeled houses in a yard in Benacre Street, Highgate, 1965. (Birmingham Library Services). J. P. Macey, Birmingham's Housing Manager, and A. G. Sheppard Fidler, City Architect, realised that this 'work is not glamorous, neither is it financially attractive, but there is no doubt that ameliorating measures of this kind ought to be carried out wherever families are compelled, through no fault of their own, to continue to live for some years in houses which are basically unfit for habitation. (*The Builder, *1955) Mr G. R. Hatton lived at 17 back of 57, Brighton Place, Abbey Street, Hockley. The date on the nameplate above the entry to the houses was 1874 and in the early 1960s 'the council came and installed fire escape hatches in all the attics, comprising of a sheet of plaster board which was to be kicked through in the event of a fire and escape via the neighbour's house.'*

Through the 'expedited completion' procedure, the council was able to speed up compulsory purchase within the redevelopment areas. This time-saving measure allowed it to take over convenient blocks of property and replan their sites whilst compensation was worked out between the owners and the corporation. Once acquired, the buildings became the responsibility of the Central Areas Management Committee, set up in 1947 to oversee the work of maintenance pending redevelopment. Around 30,000 sub-standard houses came under its control and it was estimated that it would take at least twenty years to clear them and redevelop their sites. Accordingly, the council ordered the committee to launch an extensive programme of reconditioning with the intention of making decayed dwellings tolerable to live in until they were demolished. The 1944 Act made no direct provision for improvement, nor were government grants available, so the financial burden of reconditioning fell fully on the city. Rightly it thought this expenditure was justified and the Conservative government's 1954 Housing Act vindicated the council's decision by giving government grants towards rehabilitation. Moreover, it ordered that if a local authority could not clear its slums within five years, then it must prepare schemes for improvement.

The process of soling and heeling in Tennant Street, off Bath Row and close to Five Ways, 1950s. Lily Need was one of those delighted to leave the old end. She came from Studley Street, where she was connected by kinship to almost a third of the street's people, and when she was given the chance of a house in Northfield she fell in love with the place: 'After a weekend of weighing the pros and cons, like distances from work and school, we decided to move ... Mom's brows shot up when I told her I was leaving Sparkbrook. "Whatever for?" she wanted to know ... Had she ever taken a good look at Struggling Manor, I wondered? Had she really never noticed how I'd hated the very bricks, mortar and dirty rain puddles of the place?' (Lily Need, Struggling Manor, Birmingham, 1993).

Within the redevelopment areas, sub-standard houses were improved according to their life expectancy. 'Short life' properties were those scheduled for demolition within five years of acquisition by the council. Apart from providing water supplies to some of them, repairs on these were limited to maintaining them to minimum standards laid down by the Public Health Acts. These urgent repairs and maintenance of a day-to-day nature included repairing roofs, main walls and defective drains, and making the house wind and weather tight. Intermediate properties were those with a projected survival of five to ten years. These dwellings were repaired more extensively by attending to structural problems, defective roofs, gutters and chimneys. Work on both categories was carried out by about 100 small building firms, with a combined labour force of 1,000 men and at an average cost of £40 to £50 per house. By the end of September 1953 they had given first and interim state repairs to 25,000 houses. Some indication of the enormous size of Birmingham's housing problem is given by the survival into the 1950s of this huge number of obsolete dwellings. The council was haunted by the city's unwanted heritage of back-to-backs. Even into the 1960s it was having to carry out maintenance work on this outdated and decayed type of housing.

Soling and heeling the rear of 1 back of 18, Great Russell Street, Hockley, 28 May 1948. Joyce L Boxley, once of Baker Street, Small Heath and then of Halesowen feels strongly that in the poorer neighbourhoods of Brum, 'They were really not the good old days as far as cash was concerned, but the friendliness and help every one received was much different than today. People seemed to understand and had time for one another.'

The final category of sub-standard houses were those with a life expectancy of ten or more years, and into the 1960s they were used to accommodate families who were waiting to be rehoused in more modern dwellings. Along with some intermediate property, these long-term houses were reconditioned completely. The most common renovations carried out on them were the stripping and covering of roofs, the renewing of gutters and drain pipes, and the rebuilding of badly bulged or defective sections of walls. Additionally, there was complete internal repair and decorations, external painting, and the repairing of outside water closets and wash-houses. To complement the work of renovation and to complete the process of reconditioning, the council also improved the properties. This task included supplying each house with a separate water supply and installing a separate and efficient outside water closet where the dwelling possessed its own back yard. If this facility was lacking then the corporation provided an accessible water closet to the standard of not less than one for every two houses. Of the 25,000 dwellings repaired by the council up to March 1953, 6,480 had been renovated completely at an average cost of £195 per dwelling.

Doris Rice is bathing her son, David, in the downstairs room of the family's back-to-back at 2 back of 68, Duddeston Mill Road, Duddeston. Such a room had to be living room, washroom, dining room all in one – and sometimes it was also a bedroom. The other shot shows the fireplace which is behind Doris. Living with David's granny, the Rices were just down from Parks's fish and chip shop and the 'Manor Arms' on the corner with Cato Street. (David Rice).

'Soling and heeling' was a stop-gap measure. No amount of renovation could transform a declining back-to-back into a desirable, sanitary residence. Nevertheless, the council had no alternative. If slum clearance and rehousing had started before 1914, then Birmingham's back-to-backs would have numbered less and the reminder could have been cleared more quickly. But this was wishful thinking and the council had to deal with reality, no matter how daunting or uncomfortable a prospect that was. There were 30,000 sub-standard houses in the redevelopment areas in 1947, and by 1955, 24,000 remained standing. Financially and practically it was impossible to remove them all and to rehouse their tenants in one fell swoop. From 1951 the formidable duty of supervising the job of repairs and renovation was the responsibility of the new Housing Management Department, now controlling all municipally-owned house property. Moreover, the 1954 Act meant that it would have to deal with another 25,000 obsolete dwellings situated outside the redevelopment areas. Rehousing difficulties meant that it was inevitable that these would have to be kept in use for longer than was desirable, and so standards of reconditioning would have to be highered.

Children in yard in Unett Street, Summer Lane neighbourhood, about 1965. (Birmingham Library Services). From 1950 Mrs Woodfield and her husband lived in an old back house at 1 back of 351, Bridge Street West, Hockley: 'The living room had a red quarry floor which attracted great big slugs and there were silver fish round the fire grate. The built in cupboard that served as a larder had mice. The scullery, also with its quarry tiled floor had great big heaving black-beetles and the bed-rooms had bed-bugs. All these infestations were put right by fumigating the property and regularly puffing with D.D.T.'

Soling and heeling was an interim measure. It was necessary until the building of sufficient new houses allowed the demolition of sub-standard dwellings, but attempts were made to find alternative policies. The conversion of back-to-backs appeared to be one, and in a pilot scheme eight were changed in to four self-contained 'through' houses. At a cost of £570 each the operation was expensive, but it was undertaken to provide some larger dwellings which were needed desperately for rehousing purposes. Most families living in back-to-backs needed to be moved into homes with three bedrooms, yet there was a general shortage of bigger houses which were acceptable to them. Furthermore, many residents preferred to stay in the central districts and did not want to be moved to a much more expensive post-war home in a distant part of Birmingham. Conversion was an imaginative and thoughtful action on the part of the city, but unfavourable circumstances ensured it could be only an insignificant part of its overall housing strategy for three reasons. Firstly, because it was difficult; back-to-backs were badly built and any considerable alteration in their existing walls could endanger the stability of the whole structure. Secondly, the cost was prohibitive; and lastly, conversion was impractical as it reaccommodated just four families whilst removing eight.

A smashing shot of children at play in a Birmingham yard, 8 August 1956. (Birmingham Evening Mail*).*

The council's avowed aim was to clear and rebuild its five redevelopment areas. But the city's low building rate in the late 1940s ensured that a slow start would be made to demolition. Not until the summer of 1948 were any sub-standard houses knocked down, and by March 1949 merely 270 had been removed. Despite this disappointing progress, the overall strategy of redevelopment advanced. Its principal aims were two-fold. Firstly, to separate residential and industrial property into different zones. Secondly, to reduce abnormally high population densities of 150 or more people to the acre. This would 'free up' land, thus allowing more open spaces and enabling improved road patterns, shops, services, schools and general amenities. However, the process of redevelopment itself was long-winded precisely because its objectives were so radical. It fell into seven distinct stages: design of a general layout; preparation of a programme; detailed survey; detailed layout designs; rehousing the population and reaccommodating industry and commerce; site clearance; and last of all, construction. At a cost of £17 per house, demolition was cheap, but it was one of the last stages in the operation of redevelopment and it could not begin until the city's building rate improved. This it did in the early 1950s, enabling slum clearance and rehousing to begin in earnest.

Coronation Day Party in Milton Street, Summer Lane neighbourhood, 1953. (Elsie and George Perry). Beryl Brooks lived up an entry in Vauxhall Street: 'It had no sink but a tap on the wall outside. It had gas light . . . the Brewhouse was up the yard and I used to take sack and coke and potato peelings to shovel on the fire to hot the water for the washing . . . Well by 1956 we had been invaded by rats. I went into the wardrobe and Bill's suit which was his wedding suit had the complete leg eaten. That was enough. The council rehoused us.'

Mrs Eileen Bickers with her daughters Patricia, Wendy and Valerie in front of their council house at Garrets Green Lane, Garrets Green, 1952. (Mrs Wendy Adderley nee Bickers). Mrs Smith moved to nearby Sheldon and highlighted the joys of a new house: 'We were married ... in 1946. We had to stay with Mom for two years and then we moved to 55 Bell Barn Road off Bristol Street ... as we were lucky enough to get a house, because the houses were being knocked down for the building of the flats. When we were told we were being put in a newly built house in Sheldon we were amazed and delighted because to have a garden and bathroom and all the other things we had done without for years, it was like a dream come true.'

From 1951, under the responsibility of the newly-formed House Building Committee, estates like Kitts Green, Sheldon, Shard End, Tile Cross and Lea Hall developed into huge residential areas. Indeed, between that date and 1972 the Corporation erected nearly 83,000 houses. This was a staggering achievement by any standards and was the equivalent to rehousing a quarter of Birmingham's population. Nevertheless, during the 1950s the city's progress reflected national improvements in the building of council houses. That decade witnessed an easing up of the harsh economic conditions which had bedevilled the Labour administration during the late 1940s. Fortunately, its successor, Macmillan's Conservative government, took the opportunity offered to it by prosperity and in the Housing Act 1952, it increased subsidies for building. In the later 1950s its support shifted towards the private sector, but its earlier policy reaped rewards. There is little doubt that new council houses were appreciated by the homeless and those who had lived in decrepit property. Standards of house design had dropped a little from those set down by the Dudley Report but they remained far superior to back-to-backs and better than inter-war dwellings.

New Estate on the Outskirts of Birmingham

When first we moved from Aston slums to Sheldon
The road unmade was like a country lane,
With jutting rocks and furrows of red mud
Gardens unfenced behind the new brick houses
Stretched, one vast field, a children's paradise
Of neck-high docks and thistles, bricks and planks,
Trees, tunnels, ground-nuts, brambles, dandelions.
We played and hid in half-constructed houses,
Dug dens in the soft clay, made friends,
For every family had three or four children;
No school was ready yet; all day we played
Black cinders lined the paths instead of paving slabs;
Our mothers scolded when we tramped them inside.
And for the first few weeks we had to cook
Camp-style, with saucepans balanced on the fire
Which blazed in the back-grate; our Dad
Luckily was a carpenter, so we had
Firewood, tables and a bench, which he
Rigged up for us. One of them is still there,
Painted blue, in Mom's kitchen,
While outside, where once the field was,
Privet hedges and high boards divided
The gardens neat with lawns and cabbage rows.
The concrete shopping centre in Pool Way
Which now seems such a monstrosity.
The grey rectangular blocks of flats beside,
We greeted once as signs of such modernity,
Thinking that Sheldon was being metropolised.

(Brenda Batts, Aston, Sheldon and Balsall Heath)

Neil Bradley is the policeman at the head of the parade to celebrate the Coronation in June 1953 on the Meadway council estate. Notice the two young women on the right with their hair caught up in turbans. (Neil Bradley).

The surge forward in municipal house building during the early 1950s was matched by an upswing in the construction of homes for sale. By erecting around 20,000 houses between 1945 and 1966, private builders and housing associations provided 38 dwellings for every 100 corporation houses built. Most private developments were on small sites on the edges of Birmingham, although a lot of new building took place between 1961 and 1967 on the Calthorpe Estate in the middle ring. Elsewhere, the Bournville Village Trust built many homes for purchase whilst continuing to erect houses for rent, especially as part of the Shenley Neighbourhood Scheme. This joint development with the council began in the mid-1950s, and its 580 dwellings and community facilities constituted the largest single scheme embarked on by the trust since its inception. It also leased building land to an exciting self-build project started by Harry Smith at the Austin. As house-building was still rationed by central government, its 32 members had to be given building permits from the council's allocation. Forsaking any social life, the car workers devoted themselves to the scheme and became roofers, brickies and carpenters so that by November 1955 the last house was completed. Yet, however beneficial, neither projects like this nor private building could solve the slum problem.

The Austin Self-Build Scheme, Northfield, 1955. Harry Smith was a member of this scheme. He remembered that 'for all members their new homes were something they had only been able to dream about a short time before. Some of them lived on caravan sites, these being very primitive at the time. Some were in rooms like us, some with parents with one or two children ... All this was done in addition to working 44 hours per week in the factory, plus all the travelling to and fro. (Harry Smith, Northfield)

By the early 1950s, Birmingham was building sufficient new houses to allow re-development to begin. At first sight it seemed a simple matter to knock down a slum district and rehouse its inhabitants in newly-built council houses in the suburbs. But the matter was more complicated simply because rehousing involved people and people have feelings and opinions. Sometimes a family was unable to leave the central wards because that was where its members found work. More usually, people were reluctant to move to the city's outer areas because they were unable or unwilling to pay the rent of a post-war council house. That of a municipally-owned back-to-back averaged 6s 3d (31p) a week or 9s 3d (46p) with rates, but it could be as little as 5s (25p) weekly. By contrast, and according to size, the rent of a post-war corporation dwelling was anything from a prohibitive 30s (£1 50p) a week upwards. Even if they could afford it, such a massive increase in rent meant that families from the redevelopment areas had to rearrange their financial life. For this reason the council introduced a temporary rent rebate scheme to help them over early money difficulties. Still, it was forbidding for a family to make a direct move from a condemned house to a modern property. Instead many made an intermediary move in to a pre-war council house vacated by a family who could afford a post-war municipal property.

Nellie Weir reluctantly leaving her house at 4 back of 129, Guildford Street, Lozells – her home for over forty years, 1968. A near neighbour had been Dennis Howell, later a distinguished MP for Birmingham Small Heath. (Terry Weir).

A birthday party for my cousin, Gail Martin, in front of 2 back of 15, Whitehouse Street, Aston Cross. This was the house of Our Nan, Lily Perry - Our Gail's aunt. Our Gail's mom, Winnie Martin is on the right and her brother-in-law, Freddie Hodson, is on the left. The child at the back wearing the glasses is Carol Gibbs from next door and her granny, Mrs Cheese is looking across the palings on the other side. Next to Carol is Joycie Lakin; the lad almost standing on the left is my cousin, Alan Hodson; and Our Gail is sitting on the right in the foreground alongside Our Lynne, Our Mom's younger sister. Auntie Win and her husband, Bert, were rehoused shortly after the war. She told me: 'It never entered your head to move away. I think I was the first to move away when I went to Sheldon and I used to think it was horrible. I'd be crying on the bus going home. We'd never really been on our own. You'd always got somebody's house to pop into. There was Our Nancy, Billy, Mayey, Lily all in the street.'

Despite a general desire for better houses and an improved environment, finance was not the only reason for people rejecting moves away from the city's central neighbourhoods. Familiarity was at least as strong a motive and possibly it was more powerful. Definitely, it was more difficult for the council to cope with. Officials could recognise and assist with economic disincentives to move. What they found impossible to deal with was families who wanted modern houses but did not want to move. In order to survive against the depredations of poverty, poorer Brummies had established themselves in highly-localised, closely-knit communities. Families like the Careys, Coates, Masons, and Hickmans of Studley Street, Sparkbrook could trace their residence in one street, let alone a neighbourhood, back to the 1870s and before. It was a similar story elsewhere in old Birmingham where long-established families inter-married with one another, creating close bonds of kinship within a street. Rarely did a member of a local clan move or wish to. They knew no other life, but more than that, they were aware of the support they would receive from their near and distant relatives if they were in trouble. Living so closely together in urban villages could be claustrophobic, but it was also safe and familiar. Understandably, many – especially amongst the elderly – were loath to leave its security.

BAD TIMES AND WORSE TIMES

It's true that times were very hard
When we lived in a slum with a blue brick yard.
But the money that we had was spent
On the essentials of life – food, clothes, rent.

Folk pulled together and you never saw frowns
When we went to school in hand-me-downs.

When work had gone and we kids were thin
We had our neighbours popping in,
With a bit of this and a little that,
Hardly enough to feed a cat.

But we survived and now today
I smile to myself when people say
They can't manage and times are tough,
Two cars and a telly are not enough.

But they have never lived on lard,
And played I-ackey in a blue-brick yard.
(Arthur Wilkes, Sutherland Street, Aston and Hall Green).

Karen Garry in the arms of her sister, Rita, with her mom standing by, 1962. The Garrys had come to Birmingham from Ireland and lived in a yard at the back of Park Lane, Aston. (Karen Garry).

BRUMMAGEM COURTYARD

Born in a Brummagem courtyard
which was built in Victoria's days.
The back to back old houses in crumbling old bricks,
which seldom saw the sun's rays.

Us kids played summat like football,
scored goals with some brick end or tins.
Tore holes in our hand-me-down clothing
had bruises, cuts on our shins.

And the wenches pulled dolls round our courtyard,
and they'd pat 'em, and scold 'em and nag.
And they'd treat 'em like real proper babbys,
the dolls made from sawdust and rag.

Then a man from the council decided
that all of us lived in a slum.
So they pulled down our Brummagem courtyard
and we were scattered all over Old Brum.

That's summat that people call progress,
but I'd go back today if I could,
to play marlies and tip cat, and 'op, skip an' jump,
in that courtyard in old Ladywood.

(Syd Garrett, Monument Road, Ladywood and Bartley Green)

Children outside the ramshackle shared lavatory in a yard in Ladywood, 1968. Sir Frank Price, ex-Chairman the Public Works Committee and Labour leader of the council is certain of the rightness of the p olicy of slum clearance. In 1990 he declared that 'Clearing away the stigma of 30,000 back-to-back fetid slum dwellings and other blighted and blitzed property was, and still is, one of the most fulfilling periods of my life. The fact that we had little land to house 50,000 homeless families, and over 100,000 more to be rehoused from the slums, that there were no New Towns, made our task look almost impossible. We had no other choice but to go up.' (Sunday Mercury, 1990)

Many people had well-founded misgivings about having to be rehoused, but few could disagree that the city's back-to-backs were beyond redemption. Paradoxically, their dense packing had fostered the closeness of their residents, but their bad construction and appallingly inadequate facilities sounded the death knell for the communities which had grown up around them. In many respects, traditional Brummie working-class life was born and died with the building and demolition of Birmingham's back-to-backs. The end was heralded in 1950 by the clearance of the redevelopment unit around Great Francis Street and Bloomsbury Street, Nechells. Each of Birmingham's five redevelopment areas was too large to deal with en bloc, so they had to sub-divided into smaller sections. These formed small separate redevelopment schemes and by 1953, fourteen were planned and in some stage of redevelopment, whilst four of them had been cleared of existing property and rebuilding had begun. The first large building to be completed was Queen's Tower, at the junction of Great Lister Street and Great Francis Street. It was opened officially in 1954 by the Minister of Housing and Local Government, and was one of four twelve-storey blocks of flats.

Harold Macmillan, Conservative minister and later Prime Minister, speaking at the opening of Queen's Tower, Duddeston. On his left is Councillor Frank Price and on his right is Deputy Lord Mayor, Alderman W. T. Bowen. (5 February 1954). (Birmingham Evening Mail*). Two years later, it was reported in* The Surveyor *that the proportion of multi-storey dwellings in the city's housing programme had been steadily rising over the past five years in order to get the maximum value out of the limited amount of land available in the city. It was also pointed out that multi-storey dwellings 'are more expensive and they take more labour to build than two-storey houses'.*

The clearance of Birmingham's back-to-backs was essential if a healthier and more attractive environment was to be created for Brummies. But it put councillors and planners in a quandary: where were they to rehouse those made homeless by the redevelopment schemes? These areas had very high population densities and it was found in 1953 that for every new dwelling built in them, 2.2 families had to be rehoused. There were two reasons for this imbalance: firstly, because of lodgers; and secondly, because the overall population density of the districts was lowered under the city's Development Plan. This had been prepared under the 1947 Town and Country Planning Act, and it divided Birmingham into an inner zone with 75-120 persons per acre, and an outer zone with a population density of 50 people to the acre. These figures meant that many of those removed from the redevelopment areas could not be rehoused within them; indeed, in 1955 it was estimated that about half would have to move away. Consequently, the council's predicament about rehousing now encompassed the whole city, but it found no solution in the suburbs. Quite simply, Birmingham was running out of land everywhere within its boundaries. Soon it would have nowhere left to build new homes.

Children playing outside the flats in Great Lister Street, Duddeston, mid 1950s. By this time, the housing management of the council had a waiting list of sixty-five thousand people for new houses or flats. According to Picture Post *(1956), 'Some have been on the list for fifteen years. Top priority has to go to those with large families.'*

It has become fashionable to decry the record of the right-wing leadership of the Birmingham Labour Group in the 1950s. Few now would defend high-rise flats as ideal homes for the elderly, families with young children, and others. Planners and councillors must regret, too, their unawareness or unmindfulness of the complex, localised communities which had taken so long to grow but were destroyed so rapidly. How much better it would have been if slum clearance had been more thoughtful; if neighbourhoods had been demolished one by one, allowing their families to be rehoused within their own communities. How much better it would have been if houses had been built and not flats. Yet 'if' is a great deceiver. It appears only to those with hindsight, those who can judge precisely because they have more information than people at the time. But there is little romantic in burning bugs from the attic ceiling before bed-time and nostalgia cannot thrive on a night-time walk through an unlit courtyard to a cold and uncomfortable outside toilet. Men like Sir Frank Price and Harry Watton knew this. They wanted to build quickly a better environment for their people. Tragically, they were unaware that the price to be paid was an ill effect on community spirit and a decline in neighbourliness.

Courtyard in Gee Street, Hockley, about 1965. (Mrs McLauchlan).

Part of the Kingshurst Estate, 21 November 1958. (Birmingham Evening Mail).

In 1952, A G Sheppard Fidler was appointed City Architect of Birmingham, becoming responsible for the design and layout of all municipal estates. Along with others, he realised that Birmingham was using up its available land supplies rapidly by building at low population densities. His answer to the problem was the redevelopment of mixed estates, a strategy he had pursued enthusiastically as architect to Crawley New Town. In the future, all municipal housing schemes in Birmingham would include a mixture of multi-storey flats and low-rise dwellings such as houses and maisonettes. Accordingly, high-rise flats would be built in the suburbs as well as in the redevelopment areas. Indeed, the first erected in the city were not in Nechells but in Tile Cross in 1953. Yet doubts were expressed as to the cost-effectiveness of erecting multi-storey flats. The contractor of the Great Francis Street scheme lost £57,000, and in 1954 the Chairman of the House Building Committee reported that their expense was such as to 'frighten the most stout-hearted taxpayer and ratepayer.' However, the pressure on the city's land supplies showed no sign of abating, even though in 1952 it acquired the Kingshurst Hall Estate outside its boundaries in Warwickshire. In these circumstances it seemed inevitable that the city would have to adopt higher population densities for the redevelopment areas so as to keep more people within them.

The mixed development of Kingshurst provided housing for 7,000 people and its design won a Civic Trust Award in 1963. Elsewhere in the city, the need to rehouse people on an ever-decreasing stock of land meant that blocks of flats became higher. Twenty-storey flats were erected in Newtown, and the tallest of all were the thirty-two storey Sentinel blocks built at Lee Bank. Yet as the tower blocks stretched ever upwards so too was increased the dissatisfaction and disillusion of their tenants. The euphoria of the homeless people rehoused in Queen's Tower was short-lived. In particular, they had praised the facilities within the two-bedroom flats: the large, light kitchen with the ingenious refuse system whereby everything – even bottles – could be disposed of down the kitchen sink; the good-sized living room; airing and store cupboards; fitted wardrobes and kitchen cabinets; bathroom with a hot towel rack and separate toilet; a veranda leading to the fire escape; and, finally, a drying balcony for clothing. But soon it was realised that these welcome facilities were not everything. A community spirit could not be manufactured alongside the building of flats. It had to grow and be nourished and the flats seemed to hinder that process.

Sikh workers building Cleveland Tower, Holloway Head – one of the two Sentinel blocks, 28 May 1969. In the background, is Clydesdale Tower, the responsibility of Irish frame construction gangs. The Sikhs were determined to finish before the Irish lads, and were two stories higher at this stage having started building earlier. (Birmingham Evening Mail*). The topping out ceremony was carried out on 2 June by Alderman Freda Cocks, a Conservative member of the council with a deep interest in housing and also a popular publican at the 'Dolphin' in Acocks Green.*

The strategy of mixed development on estates planned on the idea of neighbour-hood units had seemed a positive one. However, people began to recognise the faults in a policy which sought to impose a communal feeling on residents. In the white heat of modernisation and progress it was forgotten, or overlooked, that no amount of social engineering could make people know each other. Neighbourliness had to evolve; it was a gradual process based on daily contact, local knowledge and informal meetings. Living in flats made these day-to-day occurrences more difficult. They prevented the emergence of a true neighbourhood based on neighbours who were aware of each other. Residents felt isolated in their flats, cut off from their fellow tenants by a lack of unofficial meeting places. The street and its extensions had been the pivot of working-class life in Birmingham's poorer neighbourhoods. Surrounded by children playing, women had met, worked and chatted in the brew'us and the yard. They had shopped on tic in intimate corner shops, pledged their belongings in well-known pawn shops, and like men and teenagers they had gathered in casual street-corner groups, enveloped by gangs of children. Street bookies took bets, and people drank in small, familiar pubs which belonged to their street. Neighbours laughed, danced and partied, cried, argued and fought in the street. They belonged to the street. But its significance unrealised till too late, street life fell a victim to redevelopment.

Corner shop at 74, Edward Street, Ladywood, late 1950s. Eric Davies, the owner, is on the left. Next to him is his sister, Edna Kelly. Then comes their mother, Ellen Davies and a neighbour, Mrs Lawrence. (Mrs Pat Newman).

Not every rehoused person mourned the passing of their former neighbourhood. Certainly, all those moved appreciated the benefit of more rooms, modern facilities, and – most luxurious of all – their own toilet and bath, with hot as well as cold water. Many found themselves with front and back gardens and recreation grounds nearby, increasing the attractiveness of their new homes. Large numbers of them had loathed the insanitary conditions in which once they had been forced to live. On their balance sheet a vastly improved environment – especially for their children – more than made up for the loss of a close-knit community. Others viewed the parochialism of their old neighbours with distaste, seeing it as stifling and inward-looking rather supportive and safe. Whatever the viewpoint of working-class people, they could do little to halt the transformation of their city. Even the names of the Comprehensive Redevelopment Areas were altered along with their housing. Although Ladywood was retained because it was pleasant-sounding, Nechells had Green added to it to reflect the 'pleasing parkway' which intersected the district. Across the city, the Gooch Street neighbourhood was renamed Highgate, whilst Summer Lane and part of Hockley became Newtown, and the Bath Row area was changed to Lee Bank.

Children on the Primrose Hill Estate in Kings Norton, 18 May 1960. The youngsters were allowed by the council to play on the brick floor but not on the garden. (Birmingham Evening Mail). As a child Pam Woodward lived at 145, Farm Street, Hockley where 'there was no grass, just high walls surrounding the back yard, keeping it private from other back yards.' Her life and that of her five brothers and sisters 'sound as if they come from the 1930s, not the 1960s'. They bathed in a tin bath in front of the fire, slept in the attic, had to go down the cellar to fetch the coal and played on the bomb peck. In 1964 when Pam was seven the family got a house in Stechford: 'It was like moving to the counyryside. We had a front garden with grass. Lots of grass in a half circle. Large back garden. At the back of our garden was a huge field.' Still, Pam hated it at first wanting to go back to what she knew in Farm Street, 'I didn't realise this was the normal way families should live.'

Despite the increased antipathy towards high-rise flats, the council felt it had little alternative but to continue to build upwards in the 1950s. Particularly in the redevelopment areas, taller buildings increased population densities drastically, to as high as 153 persons to the acre in the Great Francis Street unit. Yet even this figure allowed the replacement of only 56% of the dwellings in these districts. In all, the population of the five Comprehensive Development Areas in the late 1940s had been 103,000 but once redevelopment was completed it would have dropped to 57,000. This meant that a surplus population of 46,000 would have had to be rehoused elsewhere. The question was, where? During the inter-war years the city had been fortunate to be able to build on large reserves of land acquired by its extension in 1911. These were no longer available and a further expansion seemed unlikely. Even the acquisition of a green-field site like the 252-acre Kingshurst estate could do little but staunch the outward flow of families from the central wards. In these adverse circumstances the council sought a solution advocated as early as 1941 in *When We Build Again*. With adjoining county councils it negotiated agreements to take some of Birmingham's overspill population. Eventually, schemes were agreed with Droitwich, Tamworth, Redditch and Daventry, and Brummies were dispersed into Worcestershire, Staffordshire and Northamptonshire. But in the long-term this overspill had little effect on the city's overall housing problem.

The playground behind the flats on the Firs Estate, 17 August 1960. (Birmingham Evening Mail*).*

Following the 1954 Housing Act, the council drew up schemes to deal with obsolescent property outside its five blighted districts, and in 1955 it defined a further fifteen redevelopment areas. With about 30,000 people, and covering around 1,700 acres, they encircled the city centre, filling in the gaps between the localities scheduled originally. Although stretching in to the city's Middle Ring, effectively they encompassed the Central Wards and most of Birmingham's back-to-back housing. Deritend, Hockley, Lozells, Gosta Green, Winson Green, Bordesley and much of Aston, Balsall Heath, Small Heath and Sparkbrook were set to be transformed, though large-scale acquisition was not possible as in 1946. Still, by 1960 the council was managing 12,000 houses in the new zones, and by 1963, 6,000 properties had been reconditioned. Unhappily, the expansion of the redevelopment programme coincided with a drastic decline in the city's building rate, which fell below 2,500 completed dwellings in 1958 and dropped to just over 2,000 between then and 1961. This was not a deliberate policy, but Birmingham's dire shortage of land meant the construction of increased numbers of multi-storey dwellings which were costlier, slower to erect and more labour intensive then house-building. Secondly, it caused the development of sites unsuitable for building because of difficulty of access, irregularity of level and shape, and poorness of load-bearing soil.

New flats in Kings Heath, 1 February 1966. (Birmingham Evening Mail). Four years later, Ray Carter, Labour MP, Birmingham Northfield, explained that: 'Most of my constituency advice bureaux are concerned with people living in high-rise flats … It is not the accommodation that worries them, but the total environment in which they live. Their health is suffering and they feel they have to get out. They are being isolated in high tower blocks and the sense of community spirit is broken down.' (Birmingham Evening Mail, 1970).

The unavoidable fall in Birmingham's building rate ensured that once again its housing register rose sharply, peaking at over 70,000 applicants in 1958. The unrelenting advance in homelessness placed the council in a familiar predicament; who should be given priority in rehousing? The slum clearance campaign had to continue apace because it was intolerable that so many Brummies still lived in ramshackle back-to backs; and secondly, because the scarcity of building land meant that the council's housing programme depended upon the provision of cleared, central sites. Accordingly, about 60% of new municipal dwellings were allocated to those made homeless by redevelopment, and the remainder to those with a high priority – especially to large families. Under pressure from the housing crisis the council adhered strictly to its rule of only reaccommodating people who had lived in Birmingham for five years. Critics believed that this policy discriminated against South Asian and Afro-Caribbean families and led to the emergence of ghettos. Certainly, hard-working black immigrants had cause to feel aggrieved at its effects, but the rule was not racial in intent. It was passed in 1949, before large-scale post-war immigration from the Commonwealth; and it was aimed at the many English, Scottish, Welsh and Irish workers who had flocked to the city recently. Given Birmingham's dire housing problem, the council felt it had to concentrate its resources not on newcomers, but on rehousing those who for years, perhaps decades, had lived in dreadful conditions.

Carmelita, Christine, Roselyn, Everton and Priscilla Jacob in their yard in Hingeston Street, Brookfields, 3 September 1969. With their father, Samuel, mother and three other siblings they had left St Kitts four years previously and come to lodgings in Sparkbrook. They had stayed there for one year, until thrown out by their landlord who wanted the accommodation. At this time, the corporation had more than 45,000 people on its waiting list for a property. The Jacobs were found a decaying house in Hingeston Street and by the autumn of 1969 were one of only four families surviving in a neighbourhood which was in the throes of demolition. There were about a dozen children left locally and 'in the rubble jungle of 1,000 hazards' these little ones 'played beneath the forbidding red "Danger" signs'. Mrs Jacobs told the Evening Mail *'of her disillusionment with modern Birmingham, of her constant worries for the children's safety amidst the crumbling houses'. Fortunately, the day on which this photograph was taken was the last in which the Jacobs had to put up with life in a small, back-to-back with no hot water and the lavatory down the yard. That afternoon they were off to five-bedroomed municipal home in Lozells and 'were full of praise for Birmingham Corporation for giving them hope for the future'. (Birmingham* Evening Mail*).*

Between 1955 and 1963 Birmingham cleared 12,347 houses in its redevelopment areas and 897 elsewhere. This was 11.5 demolitions per 1,000 of population, a ratio higher than that of Portsmouth at 8.8 but considerably lower than that of Liverpool at 27.5. This laggardly situation resulted from Birmingham's favouring of comprehensive redevelopment, but it began to improve as the rate of building speeded up under the guidance of Councillor Ernest Bond, Labour chairman of the House Building Committee from 1962. He made considerable changes in the administration of his department, and new strategies were adopted to ease the city's housing crisis. For example, the proportion of one-bedroom homes was increased, allowing elderly tenants to move out from larger houses and thus making them available for families; new types of industrialised dwellings were considered; more high-density building sites were leased from the Calthorpe Estate; and a campaign by the Liberal Councillor, Wallace Lawler, led to construction schemes with various housing associations. Still, the building rate remained under 2,500 dwellings per year until 1965 when the figure rose dramatically to over 4,000. This was thanks to the development of the huge Castle Vale Estate, five miles from the centre of Birmingham. It was located close to major employers such as Fisher and Ludlow, Dunlop, Lucas and Morris Commercial and so proved popular with existing council tenants; indeed, 78% of the estate's households were 'transfers'. However, many soon became disillusioned with a lack of community and shopping facilities, as well as with life in high-rise flats.

'Children playing in the man-made marsh that surrounds everything on Castle Vale', 5 December 1966. The shops are in the background and this spot itself was planned as an ornamental pool. (Birmingham Evening Mail). In 1989, Sir Frank Price, formerly Labour leader of Birmingham Council told the Sunday Mercury that the Castle Vale Estate had been 'built on the old Castle Bromwich airfield and I remember arguing with the then housing minister, that educated idiot Richard Crossman. I pleaded with him to keep one of the old hangars as a community centre but he gave me a tongue-lashing for being so old-fashioned. But it was madness to build estates like that without proper community facilities.'

The dominance of high-rise flats did not bring popularity and in 1958 the city's housing manager admitted that 80% of flat dwellers disliked their homes. In particular, parents with young children were fearful about the safety of living above the ground and tragically, several children did fall to their deaths. For many mothers, high-rise living became a nightmare. They were stifled and unable to take their eyes off their children in case they climbed out on to balconies or through windows which did not have effective safety catches. From 1954, in reaction to the aversion to life in a multi-storey, the council extensively built two-storey maisonettes in blocks of four storeys. Yet as late as 1965, 77% of new council dwellings were flats and at Castle Vale – where in the 1960s nearly a third of the population was fourteen or under – 60% of the homes were flats. There were other dissatisfactions with tower blocks: folk with disabilities and pensioners who found it difficult to get about were imprisoned in their homes when the lifts broke down; and there were too few facilities locally, mirroring the complaints made by tenants on new estates in the inter-war years. In 1951 in Sheldon there was one shop for every 228 residents, compared to a city average of one to 56 people. The next year the council decided that new estates should have one shop for every 100 inhabitants. Though they were to be grouped in larger centres, no house would be more than a quarter of a mile from shopping and isolated general stores would be allowed where essential. Matters improved, but in 1959 the general lack of amenities at Kingshurst led the *Evening Mail* to describe tenants there as 'Lonely Exiles'.

Mrs Denise Bennett with her two daughters, Samantha aged two and Louise aged four, standing by her kitchen window which has a faulty catch. Mrs Bennett was terrified that her girls might fall through the windows. She told reporters that although the council said the windows were fitted with safety catches she had three of them break without warning. When that happened the windows could be pushed right open. On occasions, she had caught the children sitting on the window ledges. Although a council spokesman stated that faulty window catches were repaired immediately, Mrs Bennett and her neighbour, Mrs Helen Haigh, explained that they had been waiting months for repairs. (Birmingham Evening Mail*).*

The single block of temporary shops which had to serve 8,000 residents on the Kingshurst Estate until the permanent shopping centre was built, 24 February 1959. In the meantime, many folk who wanted a variety of goods had to travel to Saltley and Alum Rock. (Birmingham Evening Mail).

From the mid 1950s, most shops on new estates were ready before the arrival of the first tenants. Unfortunately, not always were they occupied, as shopkeepers often waited for the population to increase before they opened for business. The council could not be blamed for this, nor for the lack of picture houses and other facilities provided by private enterprise. However, with local breweries it was responsible for fewer pubs in new areas and it could be faulted for a shortage of community centres. In this latter matter some people regarded central government as the real culprit, because of its close supervision of local authority developments. Certainly, the council could not be held responsible for unsatisfactory postal and telephone facilities, both of which were outside its control. Further, many complaints by tenants about life on a new estate were intangible, reflecting a sense of loss for the communities that had been destroyed with the redevelopment of the central wards. But regret at the passing of a way of life could not hide the fact that more and better houses had to be built for Brummies. In the mid 1960s thousands of people remained living in back-to-backs. They could not be rehoused until the city's building rate improved drastically. The development of Castle Vale and Bromford Bridge made this possible, and from 1966 the Conservative-controlled council continued the good work of its Labour predecessors.

Concerns about living in high-rise flats were matched by the worries of those still renting one of the thousands of crumbling properties which remained in old Birmingham. In 1967, Canon Norman Power, the vicar of St John's Ladywood, spoke out against the 'agonising slowness' of slum demolition in parts of his parish which had brought some of the remaining residents to despair. As a result, the area had been in the twilight for twelve years, with houses half-demolished and others boarded up. Amongst this dereliction lay isolated homes where the 'survivors' lived in conditions which 'have to be seen to be believed'. Through his columns in the *Evening Mail* and his book, *The Forgotten People*, Canon Power championed the cause of his people and called out for a change of policy by the council. He agreed that the slums had to go but he declared that they needed to be replaced quickly by houses and not tower blocks. His farsighted policy was ignored, as was his belief that the folk of the old ends should be rehoused locally and not moved to distant towns or estates. Canon Power was not alone in his passionate fight. In the Summer Lane neighbourhood, Wallace Lawler, a Liberal Councillor, campaigned vigorously on housing issues and for a brief time was elected as MP for Ladywood. Through their words and actions, both these Birmingham men contributed to a wider debate on the 'rediscovery of poverty' started by the investigations of Ken Coates, Peter Townsend and others. Despite the successes of the welfare state and redevelopment, they showed powerfully and poignantly that 'the forgotten Englishmen' were having to contend daily with hardship and a dire environment.

Children playing amidst the debris and boarded up houses at the back of 64, Anderton Street, Ladywood. (Birmingham Evening Mail*)*.

'Marie' in the kitchen of her council owned house in Winson Green, damned as a slum in Shelter's report Condemned. *Other Winson Green people featured in the report had no hot water or bathrooms. (Nick Hedges).*

The dire housing remaining in much of Birmingham attracted the attention not only of concerned insiders but also of commentators from outside the city. In 1966, scenes from the Ken Loach's film, *Cathy Come Home*, were filmed in Hingeston Street, Brookfields, and three years later Save the Children made a powerful short film on slum clearance. Fourteen minutes long and called *Our Generation* it sought to 'get away from the dramatic *Cathy Come Home* presentations'. Directed and co-produced by twenty-year old John Beacham, it focused on streets which were facing demolition but had not yet been fully cleared. In particular, it showed children in Ladywood playing amongst half-demolished houses and sometimes near burning debris and it suggested that the wholesale movement of folk into high-rise flats was causing other problems for children. As was explained in the *Birmingham Post on 27 May 1969*, Birmingham was chosen 'because it is one of the places where the local council has been set upon for its lack of progress in slum clearances. It has a pretty bad record.' Many in the council would have disagreed vehemently with this interpretation, but in 1971 more negative images came out of Birmingham when Shelter highlighted the slum conditions endured by families living in council-owned property in Winson Green. Its shock report, *Condemned*, looked at five other cities and it called for urgent action to rid Birmingham of slum housing which was 'amongst the worst in the country.

There was a time lag of up to two years between full clearance and rebuilding, and with such a delay much of central Birmingham was left a bleak wasteland. However, in the late 1960s – and perhaps in response to the calls of Canon Power, Wallace Lawler and others – the pace of building increased spectacularly. In 1966 the council completed 4,775 dwellings, but the next year the figure rose to 9,034. The level fell back to 7,300 by 1969, but in a four-year the total of 30,000 homes finished was greeted as a 'world record'. Under the chairmanship of the Conservative Alderman Apps, the council's Housing Building Committee rebuilt Birmingham at a rate faster than any other city in Europe, thus putting the city in the national and international spotlight. By 1967 it was rehousing 17,000 people a year and its horrendous waiting list was slashed by over half from its peak in 1958, falling to 31,506 applicants. The huge increase in the building rate would not have been possible without two factors: firstly, the widespread adoption of industrialised building methods, so that much of a high-rise flat was prefabricated and made simpler and quicker to erect; and secondly, the acquisition of a huge estate outside the city boundaries, for which the city had been pressing since the 1950s. Its pleas for more land had been rejected by the Conservative government, but in 1964 the newly-elected Labour administration agreed to Birmingham's take-over of the estate at Water Orton in Meriden. Together with the development of Castle Vale and the former Bromford Bridge racecourse, the transformation of this rural district in to the township of Chelmsley Wood enabled a final onslaught on the obstinate remnants of back-to-back and obsolescent housing in Birmingham.

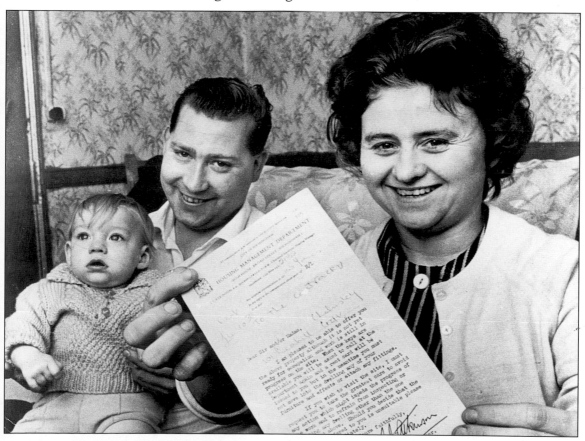

The first tenants on the Chelmsley Wood Estate – looking forward to a new home after years living in slum housing.

Almost 100 years after Birmingham's first improvement scheme, it appeared that the city's intractable housing problem was to be solved. By the turn of the 1970s the last residents of back-to-backs were rehoused and the dwellings which had characterised the city's housing stock since the Industrial Revolution were swept in to oblivion. The development of Chelmsley Wood provided the last push needed in this development. Between 1955 and 1964, the city's low building rate had allowed the council to demolish just 16,000 dwellings. Now, freed from the constraints imposed by its land shortage, it was able to clear another 22,000 in just five years between 1965 and 1969. Only 13,000 houses were left of the 51,000 the council had scheduled as unfit soon after the war, and most of the original central redevelopment areas had been cleared. After a long struggle, the city had rid itself of the bitter legacy bequeathed it by unplanned and ill-considered urban growth in the Victorian age. Well-founded nostalgia for a disappeared communal way of life could not detract from the benefits of better housing. The scale of redevelopment in Birmingham was unsurpassed by any other British city, and rightly both Conservative and Labour councillors were proud of their joint achievement. Alderman Anthony Beaumont Dark, Conservative Chairman of the Housing Committee, encapsulated their feelings: 'So far as the provision of municipal homes is concerned Birmingham has held the blue riband for the past four years and in the past three years has built more houses than any other three comparable local authorities put together. (Birmingham *Evening Mail*, 1970). But the task of rebuilding was not complete. Much insanitary property remained and by 1972 the building rate had slumped to less than 1,500 completed dwellings per year as once again building land ran out.

Ernie Goldingay (left) and George Myatt (right), site agents, studying plans for the Bromford Bridge Estate with Harry Dumbleton, assistant site agent, 1 April 1967. (Birmingham Evening Mail*).*

As usual, the city's housing register was a barometer to the council's building rate. In 1971, following the construction boom, the waiting list for a new home had dropped to 20,000 applicants; by the next year, as the building rate slumped, it had expanded to 24,000; and by 1973 it had swollen to 29,000. Yet again, the council desperately sought to staunch the surge in homelessness, and in the past its strategies were determined by the availability of building land. The situation was summed up succinctly by Alderman Anthony Beaumont Dark, Conservative Chairman, Birmingham Housing Committee: 'Land is the key to our building success and if we do not get more land on which to build on a large scale our plans to rid the city of the slums by 1975 could come to nothing. (Birmingham *Evening Mail*, 1970). Since the early 1900s, Birmingham's housing policy had been bound up with its hunger for land. During the inter-war years it was able to build houses because of the plentiful supplies of rural land swallowed up by the extension of 1911. The land scarcity of the post-war years meant that high-rise flats became the solution to the city's housing crisis, but by the early 1970s they had ceased to be regarded as the panacea to its housing ills. Most tenants disliked them vehemently and they were expensive to build and maintain – indeed from 1969, following the Ronan Point disaster, system-built flats had to be strengthened. Consequently, the development at Chelmsley Wood signalled the end of building high-rise flats on a massive scale, and only 10-15% of the dwellings were in this type of building. In these circumstances, an increase in the building rate could be achieved only by acquiring more land.

Residents of Hingeston Street, Brookfields preparing to petition the council for somewhere else to live, 2 May 1969. The lady in the centre with the white head scarf is Mrs H. Taylor. (Birmingham Evening Mail*).*

The council was acutely aware that it had to acquire rural land if it were to build houses for Birmingham's homeless and to reaccommodate those who lived in the 14,000 overcrowded and appalling slum dwellings which remained in 1972. After intense pressure, the government allowed the city to develop four sites in North Worcestershire – Hawkesley, Frankley, Walker's Heath and Kitwell. Though less than half the land it had sought, building here and at Moneyhull allowed the council to accommodate over 20,000 people. Significantly, high-density development was achieved without erecting multi-storey flats. Frankley was different, also, from other post-war estates in that it symbolised landscape architecture. Since the late 1950s there had been a move away from the 'bulldozing' approach pursued in the central redevelopment areas. Indeed, the city's Architect's Department was admired for the layout of estates like Lyndhurst (Erdington, 1958) and Primrose Hill (Kings Norton, 1963). From 1966, under the direction of J. A. Maudsley, the new City Architect, layout became increasingly important. In particular, landscape architecture was encouraged, and in 1970 the city received a Ministry of Housing award for designing the integrated community of 50,000 people at Chelmsley Wood. Frankley gave even more scope for the implementation of ideas about environmental planning.

Twenty-two year old Mrs Marie Brunn and her three children outside their home for two years in Primrose Gardens on the Hawkesley Estate, 15 May 1977. (Birmingham Evening Mail*).*

everal strategies were adopted to give a rural 'feel' to the developments at Frankley: natural features such as streams, trees, grassland and hedges were kept and houses were integrated with them; roads were not made straight but were gently curved; and homes were built clustered in small cul-de-sacs. The long rows of uniform housing of the inter-war years and the high-rise flats of the post-war period gave way to more imaginative structures: short terraces of homes were built next to semi-detached houses of two, three and four bedrooms; red-brick dwellings adjoined those of orange; tile-hung homes were by those which were wood-faced; and houses with Spanish-style windows were close to those with more traditional windows. The result was a success. Talking to Michael Pollack in the *Sunday Mercury* in 1977, Albert Cockbill said of his new two-bedroom house at Hawkesley that it was 'the best place' he and his wife, Violet, had ever lived in'. Coming from a fifteenth floor Kings Norton flat, they now had their first garden in which Albert proudly grew rose bushes and vegetable patch. Importantly, serious attempts were made to avoid the communal problems associated with previous council estates. The lesson had been learned that neither councillors nor officials could make a community spirit emerge. What they could do was provide facilities which would help this process rather than hinder it. Thus, at Frankley itself the population of 12,000 was housed in two similar-sized units, each with primary and middle schools, shops, a tenants' hall, public houses and other community facilities; and the units were separated by a broad wedge of open space, the main shopping centre and the secondary school. Unfortunately, these sensitive plans arrived as the era of council-building closed.

Edith Duffield outside her house in Frankley, 15 May 1977. Mrs Duffield said that 'I never thought I would be happy again when I lost my husband after 56 years. But it's lovely here. I haven't heard anyone complain.' (Birmingham Evening Mail).

Chapter 4:

Keeping the City Alive, Urban Renewal

A s in the past, local authority action in Birmingham during the 1960s and early 1970s was symbolic of the thrust of national policy. For much of this period both Conservative and Labour governments acknowledged the need to demolish the slums and to subsidise the building of large numbers of municipal houses. In the early and mid-1960s national and local initiatives complemented each other as governments encouraged councils to build high-rise flats and to make use of industrialised building methods. By the late 1960s, Birmingham's reaction against both these strategies reflected national concern with their shortcomings. In 1967, the Labour administration ended the higher subsidy for structures above six stories, and the partial collapse of Ronan Point led to the decline in industrialised building. Two years later, as money for subsidies dwindled, it passed a Housing Act which heralded a housing strategy based on the rehabilitation of existing dwellings rather than massive schemes of clearance and redevelopment. This trend to the improvement of older stock was enhanced by the Housing Acts of 1971 and 1974, passed by a Conservative government. The decline of council-house building in Birmingham must be viewed in the light of these shifts in the policy of national governments. Consequently, at the same time as Frankley was developed, the council implemented a programme of urban renewal.

Children playing in a derelict house, 1970.

By 1977, Birmingham's housing register had been reduced to 11,500 applicants as families moved in to new homes at Frankley and in the overspill towns of Daventry, Redditch, Tamworth and Droitwich. The council intended to keep on building dwellings, although at a rate lower than the 3,500 completed that year. In particular, prompted by the trend to smaller households, it aimed to cater for the increased demand for one-bedroom dwellings. However, its most urgent priority was to halt the deterioration of the housing stock in the inner city. The back-to-backs of Birmingham may have been removed, but that did not mean that the problem of obsolescent housing had been solved. In 1971, a survey indicated that 26,000 households had no hot water tap, whilst a further 28,000 had no fixed bath. Eight years later it was revealed that over 100,000 of the city's houses had been built before 1914. Most were tunnel-backs situated in the middle ring. Originally they had been good quality dwellings built for the more prosperous of the working class in accordance with bye-laws introduced from 1876. But by the late 1970s many of them were decaying and their facilities were outdated and inadequate. Forty thousand such structures were listed as needing either substantial improvement or a demolition and a further 26,000 were likely to become sub-standard over the next five years if they were not improved. The council had rid itself of one housing difficulty, now it was faced with another.

Serina Gall knocking on a neighbour's door in Tudor Street, Winson Green in 1970. The child's identity was not known when this photograph was published in Keeping the City Alive. *Following an appeal in the* Evening Mail, *Serina's mom, Barbara Melody, saw the photograph for the first time and recognised her daughter. When it had been taken, Barbara and her three children were living with her own mother and father and her sisters and brothers. On 18 September 1993 she told the* Evening Mail *that in all, 'there were 16 of us in the two up, two down house with no hot water and an outside lavatory . . . the housing was terrible but the community was great. Everybody helped each other.'*

Serina Gall and daughter Nikita with Councillor Matt Redmond, then chairman of the Urban Renewal Committee, at the launch of Keeping the City Alive.

Housing in Balsall Heath illustrating the decay of tunnel-back housing by the late 1960s and the need for an on-going battle against slum housing. (Birmingham Library Services).

Many owners of tunnel-back houses did improve their properties during the late 1960s and early 1970s, but as the more affluent of the working class moved from the middle ring it became obvious that fewer families would be able to afford to renew their homes. For the well-being of those of its citizens in unfit houses, it was essential that the council acted in an alternative way to large-scale clearance and redevelopment. This approach had become unacceptable for three reasons. First, it cost vast sums of money, and national and local governments no longer had the funds to carry it out. Second, there was widespread public disillusionment with a process which had taken little account of the wishes of those who lived in areas designated as slums. Demolition had destroyed deep-rooted communities and they had sundered kinship and neighbourhood networks. People were angered by their powerlessness to stop this assault on their urban villages and their frustration had begun to influence the thoughts of politicians, planners and local officials. Finally, many people from the cleared districts had been rehoused in high-rise flats. This move was resented and rejected by increasing numbers of them. These factors had serious implications for future housing policy.

The trend away from large scale demolition and redevelopment was signalled by the Housing Act of 1969. This heralded the rehabilitation of existing properties. Three years later, Birmingham City Council established an Urban Renewal Conference for Committee Chairpersons, Chief Officers and specialist advisers. They discussed how the authority should tackle its housing problems. The conference met regularly to encourage, activate and co-ordinate a policy of Urban Renewal with the intention of renovating and not clearing older houses in the middle ring and elsewhere. Of course, the short-term improvement of slum dwellings was a well-established strategy in Birmingham. It had been favoured by the Housing Committee before 1914; it was an essential response to bad property in the 1920s and 1930s; and it remained a crucial manoeuvre in the 1950s and early 1960s when sub-standard houses were reconditioned to make them tolerable to live in until redevelopment was completed. Such renovations were interim and were carried out in small areas and on houses compulsorily purchased by the council. They were not intended as a permanent solution; nor could they be contemplated as such. By contrast, Urban Renewal was motivated by a long-term vision and by the need to deal with a large number of privately-owned homes spread over wide areas of the city. In this situation, it was much more difficult to devise a way to achieve effective improvements on the housing stock of the Middle Ring. This complication was compounded by the need to make sure that the benefits of any scheme would be lasting. The success of Urban Renewal is that it rose to these challenges.

Slum housing in Birmingham, 1966. (Birmingham Evening Mail*).*

From the start, city officers imbued the concept of Urban Renewal with beliefs based on their experiences of the problems associated with slum clearance and redevelopment. The new approach was to be attached to three principles; improvement of the housing stock within the framework of the specific environment of its location; the local delivery of the services which were necessary to that achievement; and work with residents who would be affected by a programme of urban renewal via a decentralised structure. By listening to householders and making officers accountable, it was intended that policies should be informed by the concerns of local people. These guiding ideas behind Urban Renewal represented a crucial shift by the council in its attitudes and procedures. The aim was to break away from past actions which had imposed plans from above. Housing improvement was to be the antithesis of an authoritarian process of redevelopment. It was to be based on consultation and co-operation. Within a year of its inception, the Conference was superseded by an Urban Renewal Sub-Committee. Birmingham's policy and regeneration was a collaborative venture. It was co-ordinated by the Urban Renewal Officer based in the Public Health Department, directing a team whose members were drawn, when required, from a range of council officials such as planners, architects and officers from Housing, Health, Public Works and Social Services. Representing a variety of skills, views and experiences, they encouraged a multi-disciplinary approach. Such inter-department co-operation has become a model, showing the possibilities of breaking out of strictly defined administrative boundaries to make a rounded response to the diversity of problems of any large city.

Councillor Frank Carter, representative for Sparkbrook, talking to residents in Cooksey Road, Small Heath about the council's home improvement exhibition, 30 October 1971. The house had been bought from a private landlord by the corporation and then modernised to demonstrate the grants available for such work. (Birmingham Evening Mail*).*

Urban Renewal's strategy was based on two realisations: that widespread clearance was a viable option no longer – although some demolition would remain necessary where houses were beyond rehabilitation; and that the blight which had afflicted many areas of bye-law housing had to be lifted. Since the 1950s, Brummies had witnessed the wholesale change of the Central Wards. Throughout the middle ring, residents believed that their neighbourhoods were next to be cleared. Consequently, large numbers of them ceased to invest in their properties or to take up government grants for improvement (available since 1959). Their homes and districts began to look run-down and shabby. To reverse this situation both physically and emotionally it was decided to declare seventy General Improvement Areas, the framework for which had been established by new laws in 1969. These areas covered neighbourhoods where the houses were basically sound but lacked bathrooms, inside lavatories and modern amenities. Before the establishment of Urban Renewal, the council had declared nine General Improvement Areas in Witton, Handsworth, Stirchley and Winson Green. By the end of 1973, six further areas were added, including that focused on Ombersley Road, Sparkbrook. This had been developed between 1889 and 1891 when still part of the Balsall Heath Local Board of Health. That authority had enjoined the developer to construct and sewer the roads satisfactorily; it had guttered and channelled the road itself; and it had ordered house builders to erect dwellings with 9" walls, satisfactory drains and bedrooms of 100 superficial feet. Formerly a high status working-class address, by the 1970s Ombersley Road was beginning to look run down with its houses needing major repairs and improvements if they were to last much longer.

An early Urban Renewal Scheme in Clinton Street, Winson Green, early 1970s.

Enveloping a road of nineteenth-century tunnel backs, mid 1970s.

In General Improvement Areas, officers inspected every property to prepare a schedule of repairs and refurbishments necessary not only to improve it but also to upgrade it. This document was passed on to owners who were invited to obtain estimates for the completion of work on their premises. These were submitted to the Public Health Department whose officers advised householders on the amount of grant they could obtain. The city interpreted the law generously. Wherever possible, 50% grant aid was given towards renovations up to a maximum of £1,000, and in some cases loans were made to owners to enable them to cover their share of the cost of improvement. From 1974, the proportion of grant assistance was raised to 60%, whilst the money available to an individual householder was increased to £1,920. The work of upgrading a dwelling was carried out alongside environmental improvement and was not restricted to the Middle Ring, encompassing also locations of older housing in the centres of villages and towns which had been incorporated into Birmingham in 1911. Accordingly, significant parts of the outer ring were targeted for improvement in Erdington, Acocks Green, Yardley, Hay Mills, Tyseley, Kings Heath, Stirchley, Bournbook, Cotteridge, Edgbaston and Harborne. General Improvement Areas were a pioneering initiative which maximised the beneficial effects of national legislation and interpreted laws in the best interest Birmingham people. Both these features were present in the thinking which motivated Urban Renewal to declare Renewal Areas, a phrase which it coined twenty years before its use in law.

Most of the Renewal Areas were what journalists termed as 'twilight districts'. Like the back-to-back neighbourhoods of the 1800s, they were wrongly regarded as unsafe, dirty and immoral. In reality, they were homes to thousands of families most of whom were trying to cope as best they could with the depredations of poverty, ill health and bad housing. These people needed the help that was best given by investment in the local infrastructure – so that jobs could be provided alongside the renovation of houses, streets and districts. Centred on Farm Road, east Sparkbrook was a typical area of multiple-deprivation. During the Second World War the prosperous middle-class owners of its large houses had moved away to escape enemy bombing. Some of the vacated dwellings were turned into lodgings for single men attracted to Birmingham by war work. Large numbers of them were Irish, many of whom later went on to Sparkhill where they rented or bought single houses. But multi-occupancy remained a feature of east Sparkbrook, and by the 1970s it was mostly Pakistani men and other poor incomers who suffered the dreadful living conditions prevalent in many lodging houses. East Sparkbrook became a Renewal Area in 1972, as did 27 other locations from Trafalgar Road, Moseley to Trinity Road, Birchfield. Not all were characterised by multi-occupied dwellings and the presence of single men, but all did share the difficulties posed by impoverishment on a wide front. Targeted for an integrated approach to improvement, the houses and streets of the areas were upgraded within the framework of the whole neighbourhood and open spaces were provided. This strategy was novel and necessitated both close consultation with local people and collaboration with a range of Council Departments.

Brian Randle's photograph of housing conditions in Claremont Road, Sparkbrook taken on 21 January 1967. The kitchen had to be used by ten people. This area was the focus of a major study by John Rex into so-called 'twilight zones'. (Birmingham Evening Mail*).*

The Renewal Areas contained about 15,000 properties, 60% of which were likely to be unfit. By 1980 and faced with the serious and sudden deterioration of basically unsound structures, Urban Renewal had adopted a three-pronged approach: improvement; demolition of the worst premises; and progressive redevelopment. Importantly, cleared sites were to be built on with new dwellings or used to better the environment by the laying out of open spaces and the reshaping of streets. Work intended as a permanent feature was to be carried out between 1976 and 1980, but it was recognised that many dwellings required immediate and interim action to prevent them worsening further. So-called 'twilight areas' were not unique to Birmingham. There was a growing concern nationally about how to solve the ill effects of multiple deprivation and this led to three studies of inner-city areas in different authorities. Chaired by the Secretary of State for the Environment, one of these focused on east Sparkbrook and the adjoining parts of Small Heath. It investigated how physical change could improve a locality, both socially and environmentally; examined the concept of area management; and raised the questions of statutory powers and finance. At the same time, Alum Rock was included in a national enquiry made by the Home Office made into 'community development' and the closer co-ordination of national and local government with 'unofficial effort'. Such investigations and the innovative approach of Birmingham Urban Renewal informed the Housing Act of 1974. This created the legal framework for regeneration in large cities, increased the involvement of national government, and initiated Housing Action Areas. The thinking behind these resembled closely the action programmes for Birmingham's Renewal Areas and were to form the basis of Urban Renewal's work for the next fifteen years.

Mrs Maureen Ward outside her modernised home in Coplow Terrace, Rotton Park, part of the Summerfield Improvement Area, 27 October 1972 (Birmingham Evening Mail).

The majority of people who live in unfit and inadequate homes do so because they are poor. In the absence of a concerted assault on poverty itself, governments and councils have to address the most obvious symptom of deprivation – bad housing. Of course, some dwellings became unsound because they are not looked after by their residents. Such inconsiderate occupiers are a minority and should not be made the excuse for not pursuing a vigorous strategy against poverty. As a force for improvement, the Act of 1974 cannot, therefore, be seen as a solution to the housing problem. Moreover, there were difficulties associated with its provisions, such as rateable values limiting access to grant money. Some owners were unable or unwilling to pay for repairs to their premises – particularly those with lodging houses and large dwellings with high rateable values which were ineligible for grant aid. Others were inexperienced in dealing with and supervising building contracts. Occasionally, this led to shoddy repairs by a minority of unscrupulous builders, a few of whom took deposits and disappeared without carrying out any work. Another difficulty arose out of the sporadic and intermittent nature of improvement. It did not happen in a comprehensive street-by-street way. Consequently, adjoining properties could be upgraded at different times by various builders and in diverse manners. This unco-ordinated approach led to pepper potting – a clash of styles between connected house fronts, a lack of faithfulness to the original design of a terrace, an absence of regard for uniformity of materials, inadequate levels of grant take-up, and an unaesthetic look.

An example of pepper potting in Bournbrook. (Barry Toon, Community Forum).

Teresa Cloonan outside her improved home in Cromer Road, Balsall Heath, 26 March 1982. (Birmingham Evening
Mail*). The renovations consisted of new windows, roofing work, painting and brickwork and were welcomed by Walter
Rose, chairman of the Balsall Heath Residents' Action Group: 'This is an absolutely first-class scheme which is long
overdue. I shudder think what would have happened to Balsall Heath. Wholesale demolition would have meant the
death of Balsall Heath and brought tragic social problems.'*

Despite pepper-potting, much good work was accomplished in the improvement
of dwellings in designated areas. But major interests in the housing sector
remained aloof from involvement in regeneration. Building societies and other lenders
continued to refuse mortgages to most applicants from the inner city. This attitude
hindered full-scale renovation and it was essential for Urban Renewal to develop
new approaches if the work of regeneration was to be carried on successfully.
Learning from what they were doing, officers began to bring in block improvements.
Via an agency which organised the building work, a terrace of houses was improved
as an entirety. In this way, pepper potting began to be countered. Then in 1976, the
Secretary of State for the Environment announced that the Inner City Construction
Programme would make £400 million available for work on approved projects in
selected cities. The aims were to provide work in the construction industry and upgrade
targeted places. Birmingham was swift to recognise and seize this opportunity. It
launched Operation Facelift in two Housing Action Areas where no more voluntary
renovation could be achieved and where the council was about to bring into its
ownership all unimproved properties. In a fifteen month period, 769 houses were
upgraded at a total cost of just under £2 million. The improvements included the
repair or replacement of chimneys, roofs, rainwater goods, front elevations, windows
and doors. Experience gained on this project was to prove vital when Urban
Renewal initiated Britain's first Envelope schemes.

Learning from the Facelift experiment the advantages of improving whole terraces as a block, Urban Renewal began Enveloping in 1979. Under the close supervision of officers, one approved builder was appointed to carry out the external renovation of all the houses in a terraced block. Funded by money from the Inner City Partnership Programme, the process of Enveloping was tested at Little Green, Small Heath. Following its success, it was carried out more extensively on the Havelock Road scheme in Saltley. The financial support from ICPP was essential, and at a cost of £6 million, the outsides of 2,000 properties were upgraded, providing them with new roofs, gutters and windows. Significantly, attention was also paid to the environment in which a house was set with the council re-slabbing pavements, re-surfacing roads, clearing waste land, pedestrianising streets and building play areas. Although the Labour government gave a generous 90% grant towards these external renovations, many householders could not afford to pay the 10% necessary for them to go ahead. Accordingly, Birmingham's Conservative controlled council decided to pay this sum itself. The money proved well spent, and in 1979 the new Conservative government agreed with the council to jointly finance free outside improvements to 500 homes in Trafalgar (Moseley), Conway (Sparkbrook), and St Silas (Lozells). The facelifts cost £3,000 per house, and were expected to add thirty years to the life of dwellings, whilst grants were available also for internal improvements.

Improvements in Queens Head Road, Handsworth, 12 September 1983.

Internal repairs also were necessary in most of the properties in enveloped areas and improvement grants were offered to owners on pre-priced modules. This process lowered costs by enabling grants to be 'blocked' for work by one contractor and by leaving minor repairs to the responsibility of the individual householder. Single Element Schemes were another imaginative approach to renovation in the 1980s. Under this project of limited enveloping, roofs or another specific feature of a building were targeted to make funds go further. After new government legislation by the Conservatives in 1989 (The Local Government and Housing Act), enveloping ended a year later. This was unfortunate as the scheme was a great success in Birmingham. Over a ten year period, Urban Renewal had enveloped 11,000 houses. This large figure is made outstanding when it is compared with the number of dwellings affected similarly in other big cities; 2,800 in Sheffield and 350 in Bristol. Birmingham pioneered the Enveloping scheme and it made the best use of it. Undoubtedly, it had been an imaginative, effective and sensitive way of improving houses and their locations. Its success is visible throughout Birmingham. In particular it was a sensitive response to the changing ethnic make-up of much of the middle ring. By the 1970s, Pakistanis from the Punjab and Mirpur in Kashmir were settled strongly in Saltley, Alum Rock, Bordesley Green and Small Heath. Since the late 1950s they had set up strong communities based on kinship and did not want to move away from them. Enveloping then, can be seen as an imaginative and effective way of improving Birmingham's housing stock and its environment.

Mr Nazir Uddin Ahmed in the decaying kitchen of his home at 222, Albert Road, Aston. There was no bathroom, damp had led to wallpaper and plaster falling off the walls and Mr Ahmed's children were getting colds and skin infections as a result. Along with 9,000 others he was on the waiting list for a grant. Although Mr Ahmed had been told work on his property should have started in June 1984, his application was affected by cut-backs imposed by central government. (Birmingham Evening Mail).

Urban Renewal led the way in adopting an integrated approach both to the renovation of properties and neighbourhoods. Realising that in run-down districts residents needed to gain confidence in the prospect of regeneration, officers introduced 'curtilage works' – improvements to fences, walls and entries. To outsiders the sight of many new brick garden walls may have seemed uninspiring, but to residents it was a clear message of change. The walls proclaimed that renovation and not clearance was on the agenda and so encouraged general care for neighbourhoods as well as provided visible support to occupiers in their own efforts to better their homes. Such positive action was most apparent in the districts of enveloping. Officers stressed the urgent need to better the environment in a large scale and effective way and ensured that building work was carried out to a high standard, both on homes and in the street. An example of this adherence to architectural quality is the wrought iron works in Mary Street, Balsall Heath. As much attention was paid to the re-slabbing of pavements; the re-surfacing of roads; the clearing of waste land; the pedestrianising of streets; and the building of play sites for children. Throughout the Middle Ring, shabby districts began to shed their down-at-heel look as they were changed into brighter and more open-looking localities. As important as this physical transformation was the beneficial effect on householders. Many felt that no longer were they in the 'twilight' of British society.

Mr Naib Hussain lived next door to Mr Ahmed at 220, Albert Road but had seen his property improved at a cost of £10,000, 3 December 1985. (Birmingham Evening Mail*). A new kitchen and bathroom had been fitted and the house had been protected against damp and further deterioration. The Aston Resident's Association supported Urban Renewal, with its chairman, Mrs Frances Heywood, explaining that 'It's far cheaper to repair existing homes than build new ones'.*

Environmental work was restricted to enveloped neighbourhoods. It proceeded throughout improvement areas under three definitions: within the space belonging to a property – like the building of walls and making good of entries; in street renovation – as in the planting of trees along pavements, the provision of parking bays and the restriction of traffic to a single lane; and in the improvement of the general neighbourhood – such as in improvements to local shops. These facilities are vital to the life of a community and Urban Renewal recognised them as such. Such actions were everywhere dependent on co-operation and consultation. Neighbourhood based project teams emphasised Urban Renewal's commitment to these principles. Often operating from ordinary houses, as in St Saviours Road in the South Saltley Renewal Area, they became the model for Birmingham's Neighbourhood Offices and Neighbourhood Forums. Accessibility was evident in other ways: contractors displayed a telephone number on which someone could be contacted twenty-four hours a day; complaints' surgeries were held regularly; and in recognition of a need to talk to all the citizens of Birmingham, Ethnic Minority Officers were employed by Urban Renewal from its early days. A further example of care for the community was the area caretaker schemes, set up in nineteen Housing Action Areas. Funded at first by the Inner City Partnership Programme but latterly out of Urban Renewal's main-line budget, they emphasised the ongoing commitment to an area after it was improved. Caretakers had responsibility in two main fields: the good maintenance of the general environment of their neighbourhoods; and direct involvement with projects such as providing elderly people with security systems. Significantly, their duties were managed by local residents.

Nick Wigg, Urban Renewal's first area caretaker in Small Heath.

A graffiti clean up group organised by Community Forum in Bournbrook. (Barry Toon, 1992).

As a dynamic operation keen to avoid a 'top-down' approach and responsive to the worries of residents, Urban Renewal strongly supported residents' associations. Of course, there were disagreements between officers and local individuals and groups, but the decentralised structure of Urban Renewal allowed an alertness to criticisms by local people. This open nature led Urban Renewal to work with voluntary organisations – as in Balsall Heath where a farm was set up in Malvern Street, and at Hay Mills where a pocket park was created at Redhill. Such interaction was matched on a wider level by the Division's close relationship with Community Forum, a city-wide federation of Residents' (all tenures) and Community Groups. Founded in 1973, its aim was to make sure that the Urban Renewal programme should be informed substantially by the input of those who would be affected most by improvement schemes. An independent organisation, Community Forum has campaigned vigorously for the need for people to feel in control of their homes and neighbourhoods. This has meant that its voluntary officers have collected and shared information on housing, planning, the environment and techniques of consultation and have met and lobbied council departments and relevant national bodies. From its 'Cowboy Builders Campaign' in 1979 to its work with Birmingham Co-operative Housing Services to provide community led regeneration, Community Form has championed the causes of participation and self-help in housing. These objectives have been forcefully and thoughtfully put forward in two important publications: *Amsterdam, Rotterdam, Birmingham. A Tale of Three Cities* (1986); and *Clearance: The View From the Street. A study of politics, land and housing* (1990) by Frances Heywood and Mohammed Rashid Naz.

Because of its pioneering local initiatives, Urban Renewal has gained a high reputation in the world of housing. In Britain, other local authorities have sought its advice and copied its schemes, whilst Middlesborough and Newcastle have paid Birmingham to act as consultants to their Urban Renewal programmes. The dynamism and proactive nature of the city's Urban Renewal Division were essential in coping with the effects of the new legislation of 1989. This brought in more bureaucracy and regulations, swept away enveloping and made it more difficult to achieve wide-scale improvement overall. A backward step in many respects, it did provide for the designation of Renewal Areas by councils. Birmingham named four: Handsworth; North and South Saltley; and Sparkhill. Between them, these districts had a high proportion of the city's 100,000 privately owned homes built before 1919 – of which 70,000 required major renovation. Some of these properties were beyond hope of rehabilitation. This raised the prospect of wide-scale clearances becoming obvious once more. It was realised that such a process would have to be handled with care and consideration. All four renewal areas have high proportions of residents who belong to ethnic minorities; in Saltley, for example, 44% of the population has roots in Mirpur, Kashmir and a further 6% is Bangladeshi. Like the English, Irish and Italian poor before them, they have created strong neighbourhoods based on kinship and intermarriage. If their homes were to be knocked down they wanted to be rehoused in their own areas, amongst their relatives and neighbours and within distance of their shops, religious centres and community facilities.

Housing in College Road, Saltley, early 1990s.

An awareness of the needs to rehouse people locally informed the decision to make plans for the clearance of 120 dwellings in Saltley in 1992 – the biggest such scheme in Birmingham for thirty years. After discussions with other local authorities and the Department of the Environment, Urban Renewal officers submitted a proposal for a new option for householders who would be affected by the clearance. This was the Rebuilding Grant Initiative, whereby householders whose homes were demolished would be helped to buy new homes within their own neighbourhood. Impressed, the government inserted a clause into the Housing Grants, Construction and Regeneration Act of 1996 which allowed the initiative to go ahead. Once it was worked up, the Rebuilding Grant Initiative exemplified co-operation between various agencies as well as a sensitivity to the needs of householders. It was later adopted, with certain changes, by the government on a nationwide scale under the heading of Relocation Grants. The Rebuilding Grant Initiative itself included four aspects. First, the owner re-invested all clearance compensation in a new home. Second, Birmingham City Council deferred all payment for the land on which the house was to be built. Third, the city went into partnership with a housing association, the Friendship Group, which agreed to build the homes and take a privately funded equity stake in the new home and on which the resident paid rent. After a year, the owner can purchase the land and housing association's equity. In 1995, the 'New Homes For Old' idea became a reality when twenty-one houses were finished in Parkfield Road. Built by Wimpey Homes, the development is a mixture of two, three and four-bedroom dwellings.

Saeeda Nabi at her house at 91, Parkfield Road, Saltley, January 1995.

Councillor Muhammad Afzal and Broughton Road trainees. The longest-running chair in the history of the Urban Renewal Committee (1987-92), Councillor Afzal praised enveloping as marking 'an important milestone in the development of inner city regeneration'. He told the Evening Mail *(14 April 1990) that 'Birmingham can be proud that it pioneered a technique which was adopted nationally'. He feared that the end of enveloping and the new grants system introduced by the Local Government and Housing Act of 1990 'could easily see a return to the blotch pattern of improvement, and a situation where neighbours are being asked to pay vastly different amounts for the same work'. (*Construction News, *14 June 1990).*

Fresh legislation was accompanied by a national curb on public spending. This had a deep effect on Urban Renewal, dependent as it was on central government for most of its funding. In particular, the decline and eventual withdrawal of the Inner City Partnership Programme caused major difficulties as it had supported many Urban Renewal initiatives such as Enveloping, Area Caretakers, improvements to shops and grants to voluntary organisations. In these circumstances, Urban Renewal sought partnerships with government agencies and building firms to continue its work. A successful example of this approach was the Broughton Road Special Housing and Employment Initiative. The partners included Tarmac Construction, Urban Renewal, the Department of the Environment and the Handsworth Task Force, itself funded by the government and established following the riots which affected many inner cities in 1985. By renovating 38 large Victorian properties in Handsworth, the project sought to make a positive impact on three serious problems in the area of poor housing – via the techniques of Enveloping; high levels of unemployment – by way of Tarmac's use of local sub-contractors; and a lack of building skills – through the training of twenty-four young people by the construction company. Training is a feature of another of Urban Renewal's innovative partnerships, with the building firm McCarthy and Stone. Supported by a grant from the Department of the Environment, 170 homes were constructed in Trafalgar Road, Moseley. This was achieved by new building and the conversion of large dwellings into flats. The development was a mixture of houses for sale – on the open market and with subsidies – and for rent, through the Focus Housing Association. It also provided a sheltered city council housing scheme for the elderly.

Urban Renewal's fundamental purposes are to improve housing and the environment. Consequently, it is vital that residents are enabled to do things for themselves but also that Urban Renewal has the legal power to enforce improvements when necessary. Such power must be flexible. Officers face varying circumstances and need to be dynamic, adaptable and wide-ranging in their procedures. This approach is essential with regard to Urban Renewal's concern with houses in multiple occupancy (HMOs) – of which there are about 6,000 in Birmingham. They are homes to about 30,000 people, some of whom are the poorest in the city. Others are folk now living outside institutions because of Care in the Community and who may be vulnerable. Additionally, because of easier access to higher education, there has been a great increase locally in students, many of whom have to live in private accommodation. Despite landlords who maintain their properties to a good standard, lodging houses and bedsits are often dangerous, dirty and dilapidated. Their threat to life was highlighted by the tragic case of a Birmingham student who died in 1991 because of poisonous fumes from a gas fire, the flue of which was blocked by 20lb of rubble, soot and dust. Since then, Urban Renewal has sought to avoid further deaths by setting up a HMO Helpline. Overall it receives 4,000 calls annually from tenants seeking assistance. Importantly, the division has also worked with landlords to ensure the regular safety certification of their houses. This advisory service is in addition to the regular inspection of HMOs and the use of the law to bring them to proper, safe standards. In particular, legal action is necessary for hostels and bed and breakfast accommodation where homeless persons and those who suffer from the greatest disadvantages gather to find shelter.

Living in a bed sit.

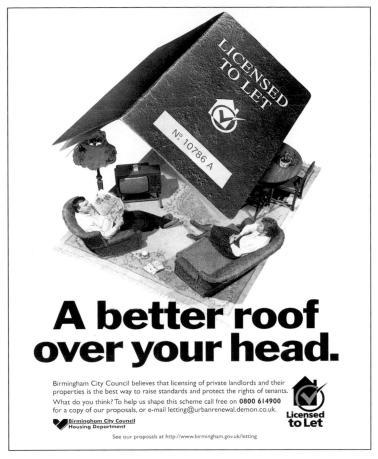

A licensed to let poster.

Since the mid-1990s, Urban Renewal has been in the forefront of caring for people living in private accommodation. It has a powerful capability to enforce the carrying out of improvements by landlords, but wherever possible it seeks to educate and persuade. In 1994 it brought out a 'bedsit card' to publicise its new Houses in Multiple Occupancy Helpline and it became Britain's first local authority to produce an Owners' Charter. This aimed to protect the rights of private tenants and to ensure that their housing was safe and healthy. Owners were encouraged to maintain their properties properly and to respect the rights of their tenants. In return, landlords who signed up to the charter were eligible for special grant aid, help with housing benefit claims and consultancy services. Since then, Urban Renewal has been active in pushing for the licensing of all privately-rented accommodation and not just houses in multiple occupancy. It has been supported in its objective by reports in the *Evening Mail* which have highlighted the poor conditions and problems at some of the city's hostels (1995). This 'licence to let' initiative was praised in 1998 by the Housing Minister and the following year Urban Renewal launched the country's first licensing scheme for private landlords through a voluntary, three-year pilot. The licence provides formal recognition for responsible landlords and helps them with coping through the mass of legislation covering rented property. It was influenced by the Private Rented Sector Forum which has brought together landlords, private tenants and voluntary groups, and by 1999 over fifty landlords had signed up to the licences.

A longside its commitment to property owners and private tenants, Urban Renewal is concerned for the housing requirements of the estimated 108,000 Brummies who have physical disabilities. Such people may require housing which is suitable to them, or else they might benefit from the adaptation of their existing homes. As in all fields of action in which Urban Renewal is involved, an inter-departmental approach is essential if appropriate housing is to be provided for people with physical disabilities. Priority cases are determined by local occupational therapists and Urban Renewal officers then work with them to design the improvements. This is followed by the commission and supervision of the works by specialist and approved contractors. Such sensitivity is as obvious in responding to the needs of elderly Brummies. In 1993 Urban Renewal launched another 'first for Birmingham' with the 'Warm, Safe and Secure' scheme. Costing £250,000 it focused on Sparkhill and Tyseley and involved British Gas visiting the homes of those aged over sixty who were home owners and receiving benefits. A full safety check was carried out and if the heating facilities were in a poor condition they were repaired or replaced. Where necessary, the insulation and security of the house was also upgraded free of charge. Pushed forward by the then chairman of Urban Renewal, Councillor Matt Redmond, as part of the city's contribution to the European year of the Elderly, the scheme was a great success. Since then, in 1998, another £900,000 was spent by the council in another 'Warm, Safe and Secure' scheme in Perry Barr where there is a high percentage of pensioner households over 75 years of age and a marked density of lone pensioners.

Miss Sandra Befour using her lift, September 1994.

Through conviction and experience, Urban Renewal has had to adopt a universal approach to housing problems, embedding them within the broader framework of society as a whole. The need for such a wide-ranging approach was emphasised in 1993 when the division commissioned a survey into 'Housing and Health in Soho Ward'. Carried out by John Kemp and Ralph Smith of the Department of Public Health and Epidemiology at The University of Birmingham Medical School, the investigation focused on a district dominated by pre-1914 private housing and with a high proportion of Brummies from ethnic minorities. Interviews were carried out with over 600 residents, of whom two-thirds complained of some sort of damp problem. There was considerable evidence to indicate that dampness caused ill health, and overall the study 'once again shows an association between perceived housing problems and poor general health, various symptoms, accidents and low levels of psychological well being'. Other findings stressed that within the home, accidents to children and adults were associated with lack of space, poorly lit homes and poor kitchen design; whilst a significant number of people had difficulties in heating their homes. Affected by the implications the chairman of Urban Renewal, Councillor Matt Redmond, argued that Birmingham needed more resources to be made available 'to enable us to provide homes fit for people to live in and improve their quality of life'. It was a similar call to that made by Reverend T. J. Bass at the turn of the century.

Improvement work at 148, Durham Road, Sparkhill, 26 September 1995.

Birmingham's first Urban Care link people in Tyseley.

The Soho Ward Report informed the thinking of Urban Renewal, as did the growing awareness that residents themselves needed to take a major role in urban regeneration. This realisation led Urban Renewal to launch the country's first Urban Care Area in 1994. Another new idea, its objective was to enable communities as a whole to take positive action to improve housing and the environment locally. Through such an approach, confidence could be increased and crime decreased. In particular, the initiative was seen as a major force in preventing the spread of urban decline to the outer city districts which had been developed in the inter-war and post-war years. Focusing on Tyseley and Fox Hollies, districts of large-scale council house building in the past, Urban Care worked at forging an alliance between residents, community and religious groups, voluntary and statutory agencies, schools, businesses, Urban Renewal and other council departments. Three inter-related strategies were evident in the new approach. The first aimed to prevent homes from deteriorating through Urban Renewal helping to set up do-it-yourself volunteer projects and by providing residents with the means to raise money to fund maintenance work. The second strategy sought to forestall the decline of the environment through the improvement of health and safety, the reduction of the use of energy, and the development of community initiatives. The third prong was through community involvement. Local people would be informed about and fully involved in Urban Care; they would be supported in their self-help ideas; they would be encouraged to manage their own neighbourhoods; and they would be encouraged to set up a community communication network.

Urban Care was based upon the realisation that increasingly problems were arising not only with houses built before 1919 but also with those erected between the wars. The challenge was how to respond to this situation given that large-scale clearance was no longer an option, that council house building had all but ceased, and that public funding for house renovation grants was becoming more and more constrained. It was recognised that ageing houses had an ill effect on the health of occupiers, they led to escalating costs of repair, and they were the catalyst for a general decline locally whereby vandalism, crime and illness rose as community confidence and house prices confidence dropped. Urban Care was seen as the fresh initiative required to break the cycle of decline. Operated by members of an Urban Care Team it has striven to include those folk who have been seen by other agencies as 'socially excluded' and it has emphasised giving power to individuals as well as to communities. According to Councillor Mike Nangle, chairman of Urban Renewal by 1997, Urban Care was 'not just about houses, it's also about building stronger communities and improving the quality of life for people in our city'. Link people were crucial in this process. These are ordinary citizens who volunteer to pass on and update information on a variety of local services promoted by the Housing Department. In particular, they receive material on home improvement, support for the elderly, home safety, health, security and community projects.

Videoing for the production of a home maintenance video for Urban Care, 1994.

Sitting down in the Sparkhill Community Shop is Derek Harrison, Urban Care worker. Standing by him are Jack Rivett, a well-known activist in the local community, and a customer, March 1998.

Urban Care has made a major impact on Sparkhill in particular. In 1995, it was the setting for the 'Stitch in Time' home maintenance scheme which was heralded by the opening of an exhibition caravan. Here and via meetings with residents association representatives, newsletters and information sheets, residents were shown how to make their homes safe and how to save large repair bills in the future by acting effectively in the present. Importantly, the message was reinforced and sustained by a technical officer who gave maintenance advice to residents in their own homes. Following this, the officer was enabled to schedule improvements, assist with prioritising them, and connect residents with local schemes to the community builders list so that reliable contractors could be employed. Such self help was the over-riding feature of the Health Help project which had been started three years previously in Sparkhill with funding from the Inner City Partnership. Established by Sparkhill residents with the help of Urban Renewal, it worked by linking people in need with local volunteers who could give help and advice. In a three year period from its inception, the scheme led to over 600 home safety checks and the fitting of 1,556 security items and more than 900 safety aids to homes. The growing pride of Sparkhill people was emphasised by the setting up of a Community Shop in 1994 at 518 Stratford Road. The result of the ambition of residents groups, it offers practical help for elderly and disabled residents, and provides educational and training support to help meet local employment needs.

Significant aspects of Urban Care are the establishment of tool loan schemes, bulk buying, skill swap schemes and a community builders list. Since its inception, the division had been careful to employ good quality builders and had set up a list of 175 approved contractors. Over 90% of these firms were based in Birmingham and employed local people. In 1994 Urban Renewal reinforced its commitment to good building practice by initiating an annual Good Contractor Award Scheme which recognised consistently high standards of work and customer care. The initiative was supported by the Federation of Master Builders which had close contacts with Urban Renewal and which had agreed a 'Builders Code of Conduct' with the city. In its backing for reputable contractors and the campaign against 'cowboys', Urban Renewal also began to establish community builders lists managed by community associations with guidance and support from the division. Then in 1997, for the first time it released its list of approved private builders to the public free of charge. Again the move was supported by the Federation of Master Builders and the following year the council sent out over 1,500 copies of the list following a major campaign by the *Evening Mail* against shoddy workers carrying out inferior building repairs. The publication of the private builders list of reliable contractors was central to the success of Urban Care in November 1998 in winning the National Home Improvement Council's annual competition to find the best new innovation in the private sector by a local authority.

Builder Paul Harris who, together with his brother Thomas, was awarded a special award of merit in the 1998 Good Contractor Awards. Trading as P.E. Harris the King's Heath-based company was the first to win a Good Contractor Award in three successive years.

Junior SRB members with the then vice chair of the Urban Renewal Committee, Councillor Abdul Malik.

In the face of declining financial support from central government and with demand for grants outstripping the available money, Urban Renewal has needed to hone constantly its innovative skills so as to be able to continue its essential work. In particular, it has needed to respond to legislation which means that grants are no longer mandatory. As a consequence, the division has needed to adopt a new points system for allocating house renovation grants. It was decided to focus on the condition of the property and the circumstances of the occupants, with especial consideration given to families with very young children, pregnant women and the elderly. At the same time, Urban Renewal has actively sought involvement with Single Regeneration Budgets (SRB), seeing in this development significant connections with Urban Renewal policy. In competition with other councils, Birmingham won £23.5 million for new projects to improve the lives of residents in Sparkhill, Sparkbrook and Tyseley. The money was to be spent over seven years and Urban Renewal was to be responsible for £6.5 million. This was to be used for improving homes especially on the Barber Estate; helping with local environmental problems; boosting property maintenance by home owners; and improving health and safety within the home. Approval for the first £15 million worth of projects was given in September 1997. Put together by Birmingham Partnership, a coalition of community organisations and the public and private sectors, the projects had been developed with local people and were to be managed through the SRB Board. In addition to 2,0000 new jobs and 10,000 training places, the proposals envisaged 3,000 new and improved homes.

The positive effects of Urban Renewal are obvious. By 1993 the division had been responsible for 20,000 improved houses, as well as 11,000 which had been enveloped; 40,000 properties had been covered in 94 General Improvement and Housing Action Areas; 7,700 dwellings had been encompassed in Renewal Areas; and 53,100 homes had been renovated with individual grants. These figures make Birmingham Urban Renewal the most active and progressive organisation of its kind in Britain. But it is marked out by more than its physical improvements. Statistics tell a story about houses, but Urban Renewal is for people. In planning and providing its services, it is characterised by its attentiveness to people. Residents' Associations have been set up; booklets and cassettes have been produced in South Asian languages; and special services help householders by filling grant forms and supervising renovation. Urban Renewal is an ongoing process. It can never end. Of Birmingham's private-sector housing, 16% is unfit as defined by law, more than twice the national average, whilst a further 80,000 properties are 'borderline unfit'. Overall, it is estimated that it would cost £750 million to repair and improve this housing stock. And it must be borne in mind, that unsound homes are not just those built before 1919. Age is beginning to have an adverse effect on the third of Birmingham's dwellings erected in the 1920s and 1930s. Their deterioration will have a significant effect on Urban Renewal in the future. That difficulty has been recognised in Birmingham. It needs to be noticed as much on a national level.

Mrs Guzin Lone and her son Adeel pictured outside their home in Ludlow Road, Saltley in 1991 moments before the then Housing Minister, Sir George Young, arrived on an official visit to see their home being improved by Urban Renewal.

Chapter 5:

Regeneration and Empowerment, Council Housing Since 1979

O ut-of-date dwellings are not restricted to inner-city areas and in 1979 the council began a huge ten-year plan aimed at the modernisation of the 30,000 ageing inter-war council houses with 'antiquated facilities'. Following the recommendations of Richard Westlake, the city's Housing Officer, this was approached in a coherent and comprehensive fashion. Instead of tackling it piecemeal on a scattered system, it was carried out on a street-by-street basis, tied in to planned maintenance. Modernisation involved repairing the fabric of the house where necessary, for example putting on a new roof; rewiring; enlarging the kitchen to provide a kitchen-cum-breakfast room in non-parlour houses; and moving the bathroom upstairs. On average, it cost £5,000 per house and put 60 to 65p on rents, and whilst it was carried out tenants were moved temporarily – usually for eight weeks – into "decent" houses. Part of the reconditioning strategy included the conversion of some inter-war houses into two self-contained, one-bedroom flats. This allowed elderly tenants to stay in their area, freed up houses elsewhere for families, and gave accommodation to single people who were now admitted to the housing register. Subsequently, in November 1998, the council carried out a wide-ranging review of its general repairs policy informed by the knowledge that over 500,000 responsive repairs were carried out annually to the detriment of a planned approach to long-term maintenance. The new procedures mean that the council will emphasise those repairs which it has a legal duty to carry out, whilst the renewal or repair of minor items becomes the responsibility of tenants. This shift fits clearly into Urban Care and is an obvious example of the coming together of the Housing Department and Urban Renewal.

Steve and Deborah McBride with two of their children, Michelle and baby Jason, outside their maisonette in Lawden Road, Bordesley, 1985. Along with the majority of the tenants on this, the Spring Vale Estate, they were hoping that their homes would be demolished. (Birmingham Evening Mail).

Mrs Jeanne Wakefield and her bottle of sterra about to enter the caravan in the front garden of her house in Jervoise Road, Weoley Castle, 5 February 1979. (Birmingham Evening Mail). Faced with the need to improve over 30,000 of its own properties, the Housing Department also realised that many tenants did not wish to move into temporary accommodation whilst the work was carried out. Consequently, fully-fitted portable caravans were provided for residents. Like many others, Mrs Jervoise was pleased with the strategy. She told Roland Smith of the Evening Mail *that, 'It has two advantages. The tenants are not put out, and the job gets done quicker.' Each caravan cost £20,000, whilst the renovation of each council house was £7,000. The work included a complete re-wiring, the fitting of partial gas central heating, and installing a new bathroom and fitted kitchen. Mrs Preece, another Weoley Castle tenant, thought that the council 'had bent over backwards to be kind and helpful'. In her case, her rent for a three-bedroom semi-detached house rose by about £1.50 a week from £9.*

Any hopes that councillors and Brummies have had that the city's housing problems have been solved seem to be dashed with a monotonous and unrelenting regularity. Each decade of the post-war years has been associated with a particular housing worry. The 1950s and 1960s were marked indelibly by the struggle to eliminate the city's back-to-backs; the 1970s and the 1980s were scarred by a need to grapple with the problems of shrinking investment and a worsening housing stock in the inner city and on inter-war municipal estates. Unless central government grasps the nettle of bad housing, then the first decade of the new millennium may be marred by the mounting difficulties posed by the legacy of high-rise flats and flawed industrialised building techniques. Indeed, the tocsin warning of the imminent approach of a new housing dilemma was sounded in 1979, when it was decided to demolish the pre-war St Martin's flats in Emily Street, Highgate. Built with such high expectations just over forty years previously they were now unpopular and regarded distastefully as a 'rambling run-down warren of 266 problem flats' (Birmingham *Evening Mail*, 1979). Their short and undistinguished life indicated the enormity of the predicament created by Birmingham's 429 blocks of post-war, multi-storey flats. By February 1999 clearance had reduced this figure to 360. Of this total, many are affected by structural defects often associated with the non-traditional building techniques used in their construction. Similarly, by the late 1980s, hundreds of inter-war houses which were also built non-traditionally were crumbling and disintegrating as long-term chemical reaction and weathering affected substances like colliery waste which were used as aggregates in their building.

The clearance of the St Martin's Flats, Emily Street. The buildings were finished in 1939 and demolished in 1981. (Birmingham Library Services).

In 1985-86 an abseiling survey revealed grave problems with many of Birmingham's tower blocks. Amongst the most serious was the loosening of cladding panels due to rusting metal ties and the effects of the weather. Falling masonry can result and so many multi-storey flats have been surrounded by temporary fencing and scaffolding to prevent walking in hazardous places. Elsewhere, tenants are plagued by serious dampness or have no long-term security because potentially defective concrete frames and bases may lead to demolition. The cost of repairing the worst affected flats is often upwards of £50,000 each, the price of a new three-bedroom house, and it would add thirty years to their life. Even so, demolition might be the most effective solution financially and socially, and a number of blocks have been knocked down on these grounds. Yet if clearance may be desirable it is not necessarily advisable. Tower blocks house thousands of tenants and where would they live if their homes were destroyed? The Conservative government's popular Right to Buy policy brought home-ownership within reach of many working-class people but it meant the annual reduction of council-owned dwellings, especially the most popular of them. In April 1980, six months after the new initiative began, Birmingham's housing stock was 136,005. By February 1999 it had fallen to 93,384. Of this figure, 45,646 were houses (48.6%); 39,011 were flats (41.6%); 4,996 were maisonettes (5.3%); and 4,253 were bungalows (4.5%). Some of this drop came from the transfer of Castle Vale to a Housing Action Trust and by increased clearance, but the greater part is through Right to Buy. With fewer properties available each year for transfer, the council has found it more difficult to meet the housing needs of its tenants and of those seeking a corporation property – especially of a family house.

One of the engineering inspection team from Can (UK) Ltd employed by the council to carry out an abseiling survey at a cost of £300,000 on the city's tower blocks, 4 June 1985. (Birmingham Evening Mail*). This engineer is coming down one of the Sentinels on Holloway Head. By this date, 135 buildings had been inspected, two of which had to be evacuated and another 78 had to be fenced off.*

Under both Conservative and Labour-led councils, Birmingham strove to diminish the likelihood of the severe housing crisis threatened both by the increasingly evident structural flaws of high-rise flats, and the social problems associated with them. In 1979 it inaugurated a plan which aimed to encourage elderly people to move out of under-occupied council houses, so allowing swaps with families with children who lived in flats. The two blocks first converted were in Grove Road, Kings Heath, where sixty-seven flats became warden-service homes. Each was fitted with an intercom alarm system linking the tenants with the warden, an entry-phone network was installed to keep out vandals and intruders, and all the residents had use of a community room. The pioneering flats cost £40,000 to convert in what was believed to be the first scheme of its kind in the country. They have proven popular with the elderly and in all 45 blocks have been converted into vertical warden schemes, whilst a 'concierge' scheme has been introduced in 44 other blocks. In addition, there are two single person blocks and nine maturity blocks. Another strategy adopted by the Housing Department with regard to multi-storey buildings has been to lop off the top two floors of four-storey maisonettes. This has created two-storey houses, as at Bennett Street and Johnstone Street, Lozells in 1983. However, not all high-rise blocks can become warden-serviced, and most are too high to be suitable for lopping off. Furthermore, many of them are so unsound structurally that any form of conversion is most unlikely.

The Concierge Scheme at work, 1990s.

Throughout the 1980s, many tenants were faced not only with deteriorating housing conditions but also with social problems exacerbated by a deep economic recession. From the late 1950s, the more prosperous of the working class had begun to buy their own homes and move away from council estates. Consequently, some areas gradually became dominated by older folk or those on low incomes. This shift in the demographic pattern amongst municipal tenants could have serious repercussions, as was made apparent in 1987 by the report 'A Picture of Health'. Compiled by the Department of Community Medicine in the Central Birmingham Health Authority, it analysed sickness and death rates on the wards it encompassed. In particular, it gave information on two different areas which were seen as poor. The first was Nechells and Duddeston, where 87.5% of the property was owned by the council and the population was mainly white and Afro-Caribbean. Its unemployment rate was 38%, and there was a high proportion of single parent families. The second was Sparkhill, where only 7% of the dwellings were municipal and there was a South Asian majority. Here the unemployment rate was 30% and there were more over-crowded houses. This latter problem meant that Sparkhill had a higher incidence of chronic lung disease, whilst strokes were also more prevalent than in Nechells. By comparison, in Nechells, infant mortality was twice as high as it was in Sparkhill, whilst all childhood deaths and deaths for from all causes in the 15-64 age group were also more marked. Overall and allowing for difficulties with exact comparisons, as Francis Heywood and Mohammed Rashid Naz pointed out, 'Nechells, with its post-war council housing, emerges as a place where health is in general worse than Sparkhill with its Victorian terraces'.

Roy Read, chairman of the Bloomsbury Estate Management Board which is playing a vital role in the regeneration of much of Duddeston and Nechells, early 1990s.

Tenants in a high-rise block in Duddeston taking part in the Secure by Design project in conjunction with West Midlands Police.

In the mid 1800s, Greens Village was feared as a place in which lived a violent, drunken and criminal population. My own research into the Irish of Birmingham has shown that this negative image was constructed by middle-class outsiders who knew little of the neighbourhood or else wished to see it cleared for their own ends. Similar demeaning attitudes were later held of Summer Lane and other poorer neighbourhoods in Birmingham. In reality, these districts were characterised by tightly-knit communities bonded by loyalties to family, kin, neighbours and street. Of course, amongst the poor there were those who were disreputable and reprehensible – but such people were also to be found amongst the upper and middle classes. Unfortunately, today many council estates are denigrated in the same way as were Greens Village and Summer Lane. Little notice is taken of the majority of residents who are decent, respectable and hard working. That is not to ignore the problems faced by such folk on an estate where harmony is constantly strained by a high proportion of tenants who stay for only a short time and hinder the emergence of a fully settled community. This phenomenon often leads to a loss of respect for neighbourhoods manifested by vandalism and graffiti. Crime overall has also been exacerbated by badly-designed buildings and estate layouts. According to Ted Schuck, a former police officer and by 1989 a civilian projects officer in the West Midlands crime prevention department, 'many of our estates have indefensible space which belongs to no-one and is taken over by undesirables . . . . The houses and flats tend to have secluded entrances, are connected by rabbit-run type alleyways and are poorly lit.' These factors attracted muggers and burglars and could contribute to sending an estate into a spiral of decline.

Often as much as crime itself, the fear of crime had invidious effects on tenants in certain estates and heightened social and individual isolation. In turn, this exacerbated a lack of commitment to a neighbourhood. This unfortunate situation occurred when transfers were becoming harder because of a decline in council house building and the drop in municipal properties because of the Right to Buy. Many people have benefited from council-house sales and a positive expansion in home ownership. Yet not everyone can afford to buy a house and such folk have found it increasingly difficult to look towards councils for their accommodation needs. From 1979, successive Conservative governments diminished the role of local government social housing and through complicated rules effectively prevented the spending of money gained from sales. The serious effects of these policies were made plain in 1988/89 when Birmingham council completed just twelve new homes. Council house building may be desirable, but financial restrictions make it unlikely. Consequently, the Housing Department must continue to be innovative in responding to housing problems and the demand for community-based housing solutions. Few could argue against consumerism in rented housing with its aim of giving council tenants more control over their homes and environment. Still, if it is to be successful then councillors and housing chiefs have to indicate their willingness to listen to tenants and abandon concepts of imposed social engineering previously so popular amongst planners. If the Conservatives might be faulted for their aversion to council house building, they can be seen as enabling the empowerment of municipal tenants. This shift became obvious in 1992 when councils were forced to put their housing management services out to tender. This move allowed private companies, housing associations and tenant management organisations to take over the running of corporation estates.

Tenants viewing property in and around Rake Way, off Tenant Street, near to Broad Street

Faced with the effective loss of its ability to build houses, the council recognised the need to work with other agencies to bring in their expertise and resources in order to tackle the city's housing problems. In particular, close connections were sought with housing associations which now have a major role in meeting the needs for rented accommodation. Indeed, these organisations have provided nearly half of all new homes built in Birmingham since 1988. One of the earliest examples of a joint initiative came with the response to the problems of the Stockfield Estate, Acocks Green where families living in defective housing voted for the demolition of their 477 crumbling homes. In response, the Housing Department created a national first in setting up a local housing company, the Stockfield Community Association, to redevelop the estate. This is made up of two companies. The parent company is a registered non-profit making charity and focuses on providing houses for rent. Its homes are built by the subsidiary company which is a general trading company. This structure allowed new quality homes to be built outside the financial constraints placed upon the council. The association has overseen the building of 425 new homes of mixed tenures in a £24 million development in partnership with Bromford Carinthia Housing Association, Wimpey Homes, architects Webb Seeger Moorhouse, Anthony Collins Solicitors and the Halifax Building Society. Rebuilt in stages, the project was completed in 1998. The council's partnership and innovation in forming the country's first community association was recognised by an award from the National Housing and Town Planning Council in late 1996.

Councillor Mike Nangle and residents looking forward to the demolition of the Stockfield Estate.

Local residents celebrating the beginning of the regeneration of Pype Hayes. Left to right are: Hilda James, Councillor Stan Austin, Mike Sharpe, Jo Cooley, Robin Corbett MP, Brenda Watts and Sid Marks.

Derek Waddington, Director of Housing in the early 1990s, felt that community-based schemes like that at Stockfield provided new opportunities for sensitive yet realistic housing policies for the coming decades. Certainly, regeneration through partnerships with residents, housing associations and private enterprise has become a key factor in the redevelopment of other council estates, such as that at Pype Hayes. Six miles to the north east of the city centre, the neighbourhood covers about 110 acres consisting of 1,368 Boswell Homes built in a non-traditional manner. Designated as defective under the 1985 Housing Act, the properties were demolished and the estate comprehensively redeveloped. This change was co-ordinated through the Pype Hayes Steering Group, formed in 1990 from residents representatives, their consultant, local councillors, the MP, and council officers. In consultation with the local community the group developed the Pype Hayes Concept Plan which was approved by the council in 1992. This broke the estate into about twenty sub-areas which would be developed in phases. The main objectives of the plan were to create a place that was attractive to live in; accessible and comprehensible to residents and visitors; and safe for local people to live in and move around. The Concept Plan incorporated the creation of an estate characterised by a low rise, high quality homes of different types and tenures. Environmental concerns would be addressed by a low speed, low volume traffic environment; the adequate provision of off-street street parking within the curtilage of each new home; the restriction of access to heavy goods vehicles and 'rat run' traffic; the rationalisation of public open space via redistribution and a higher quality design providing amenities sought by the local community; and lastly, the creation of a green corridor through the estate linking the Birmingham Fazeley Canal to Pype Hayes Park.

Council Bungalows at Pype Hayes.

Almost a decade later, the redevelopment of Pype Hayes is well advanced and will be completed in 2002. Urban Design has been a fundamental feature in this regeneration. Detailed thought has gone into the formation of good routes and paths, creating a sense of enclosure and of places, treating edges and boundaries, the types of corners, enhancing privacy and security, exploiting landmarks and views, making liveable streets, and working with nature. In attending to these concerns, sight was not lost of the importance of good housing which was well designed and imaginative. Throughout, the feelings and opinions of residents were paramount. A local project office was set up with its own dedicated housing team and an editorial board was convened to produce *PypeLine,* a regular estate newsletter dedicated to ensuring that residents knew what was going on. Significantly, residents elected their own representatives who participated in each stage of the project and approved layouts, house types, internal arrangements of dwellings, elevations, street scenes and specifications. On the building front, land was marketed to Wimpey Homes, Beazer Partnership Homes, Lovell Partnerships and Fairclough Homes, and the Waterloo Housing Association. In return the council gained new municipal housing and the agreement that for every six houses erected for sale there were four constructed for rent. Over a quarter of the original residents have moved into these rented homes. In its approach, the Waterloo Housing Association allowed new tenants to make choices ranging from the plot for their house to the colour of their kitchen cabinets.

The outstanding partnership work and innovation the Housing Department had demonstrated were validated at the National Housing and Town Planning Council Partnership Conference in 1998 when the Pype Hayes Estate was voted the outright winner in this prestigious national competition. This success for one of the biggest housing developments in Europe was achieved in the face of strong competition from 70 other schemes from across the nation. The Housing Department also received a commendation for its work in Perry Common, where 908 non-traditionally built 'Boot' houses are being replaced by new homes constructed for the Witton Lodge Community Association, Birmingham's second local housing company. The partners in the project are the Servite and Bromford Carinthia Housing Associations. Residents have decided which parts of the estate should be redeveloped first and as in Pype Hayes, the community effectively is leading the regeneration programme. A further commendation was gained for partnership work with the Bournville Village Trust and the Birmingham Heartlands Development Corporation in Bloomsbury. Part of Birmingham's first post-war redevelopment scheme in Duddeston and Nechells, Bloomsbury was regenerated through five stages. These involved the demolition of structurally unsound and unpopular blocks of flats and the sale of sites to housing associations and commercial house builders so as to allow the construction of traditional family houses. Grant aid from the Heartlands Development Corporation helped to provide shops, offices and new medical facilities, whilst the ultimate control of tenants was ensured by the Bloomsbury Estate Management Board – itself another national first. Once again, a main feature has been the movement back into the area once new homes were available. With nearby Bordesley, Bloomsbury is widely viewed as a prototype of the urban villages which are likely to be key features of regeneration in the future.

Outside Lee Bank Neighbourhood Office, Joy Aldworth is publicising Neighbourhood Forums – bodies open to all residents and operating in a manner similar to that of residents' associations, mid 1990s. Representing the Sparkhill Springfield Neighbourhood Forum, Joy was with Albert Russell of Stockland Green Neighborhood Forum (back row right). Bert Thorpe in the front and his colleague on the left at the back were representing Housing Liason Boards – bodies aimed at giving council tenants a voice.

Shops and flats on the Lee Bank Estate, early 1990s.

Birmingham has been successful in bidding for new sources of government money such as the Single Regeneration Budget (SRB) Award of £23 million to initiate regeneration projects in Sparkbrook, Sparkhill and Tyseley. As part of this, the Housing Department decided to carry out extensive improvements in the Highgate neighbourhood, close to the markets quarter and south of the city centre. In 1994, it had about 4,000 people and higher proportions of younger residents and single parent households than the averages for Birmingham as a whole. The majority of households – 74% – lived in council accommodation with only 15% in their own property compared to a city-wide average of 60%. There were 1,752 dwellings of which 80% were flats or maisonettes. From 1992, tenant involvement in local housing matters, policy and the introduction of more open and accessible decision-making processes were promoted through a local Housing Liaison Board. Amongst the issues most often brought up by tenants were structural problems in multi-storey blocks, lack of security, badly sited and outdated children's play areas, poor lighting, and inadequate noise insulation. After extensive consultation with residents, £7.5 million from the SRB budget was allocated to provide properties with new roofs and windows and to carry out environmental improvements for parking and gardens. Supplemented by £4 million from the council, the schemes also includes demolition of outdated maisonettes and the building of new houses. The council has continued to manage the properties, but through local arrangements tenants are able to have an effective voice in development and to exercise choice as to how investment is targeted within their neighbourhood. Significantly, Highgate was chosen for the pilot to assist tenants in coping with their new repairs responsibilities.

Housing Liaison Boards are a significant opportunity for residents to influence the running of their own areas in conjunction with the Housing Department and other council organisations. Irene Brown is an active member of her board in South Aston and has listed over forty of its achievements, an indication of the way a buzz word such as empowerment can have a real meaning in day-to-day life. Amongst them are the funding obtained from City Challenge for two tenant management officers; the provision of new lifts for two tower blocks; and improvements to the frontages of property in Park Lane. The HLB has also been successful in forging close liaisons with the police, lobbying for a regular street cleaner, compiling an estate profile to underpin a capital bid by the Housing Department, and putting together a dossier on crime for the Chief Constable. Irene and the other HLB members reflect the concerns of other local residents and most often have focused on four main priorities: crime and safety; housing; environ mental mattress; and community facilities. Such a wide-ranging approach to their neighbourhood emphasises that housing cannot be separated from other social issues. Recent HLB 'victories' have included having the traffic lights moved from the middle of Victoria Road to the corner of Upper Sutton Street and Victoria Road 'where they should have been in the first place'. Members also 'kicked up a right stink at the local ward meeting when we were informed that the Planning Department was proposing to remove a perfectly sound palisade fence surrounding the area ear marked for the new community centre in Upper Sutton Street'. The planners intended to replace it with an inferior fence to complement the fence recently erected at Aston Tower School, at a cost of £42,000, 'when we were desperately trying to raise capital for CCTV cameras.'

Irene and Tom Brown have devoted many years of their life to working for their fellow residents and improving their neighborhood in Aston. Sadly, in the spring of 1999 they were mugged and badly beaten. The attack has not bowed them down. they are determined to keep on acting as good citizens.

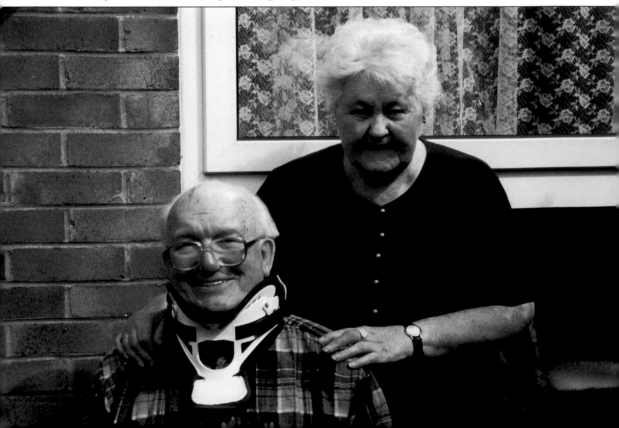

The Cadbury Drive site on the Castle Vale Estate, showing new low-rise houses in the foreground, October 1997. Developed by the Castle Vale Housing Trust they contrast sharply with the high-rise blocks in the background which will soon be demolished. (Castle Vale Housing Action Trust).

At the start of the 1990s, David Cowans, then Deputy Director of Housing, suggested that the ensuing decade would be one 'of increasing consumerism in housing services which will mean the need to provide more and more choice for people not only in terms of the tenure of their home but in terms of the quality of services they receive'. This consumerism has been evident in the regeneration of Castle Vale. In 1993 and with the support of the council, its residents voted to opt out of municipal control and become a Housing Action Trust. In such a case, rebuilding and improvement are overseen by a board consisting of four tenants, two councillors nominated by the city, and five nominees of the Environment Secretary. Similarly in 1998, tenants on the Benmore, Lee Bank and Woodview Estates voted to transfer from the council to a non-profit main landlord. This was Optima Community Association, a new registered state landlord sponsored and supported by the city. Tenants have seven members on the fifteen member board which is responsible for a grant of £46 million from the Estates Renewal Challenge Fund and for private loan finance approaching a further £40 million. The mechanics of control in Lee Bank and Castle Vale differ from those in Highgate, Stockfield, Pype Hayes and Bloomsbury but all the controlling bodies have certain over-riding aims in common. They want to make life safer for residents, to design attractive estates which will enable the building of settled communities, and to allow residents real control of their communities. As Graham Farrant, Director of Housing, has affirmed: 'Birmingham is listening to what residents are saying'.

Aware of the need to embrace a more strategic role in the future of housing, the Housing Department and Urban Renewal came together in 1997. With the drastic reduction in council house building and an acknowledgement that residents needed to be empowered if regeneration were to be successful, the overlap between the two organisations was more obvious. Both were concerned with improving housing conditions. Both were pledged to work for a better environment. Both were committed to co-operating with residents for and on behalf of residents. Both were alert to the need to seek partnerships with other agencies. And both were keen to innovate and adapt to attain their objectives. They have achieved much in the 1990s but more remains to be done. In housing terms, Birmingham is the fifth most deprived local authority in the country. Many estates need to be regenerated; the population drift from the city has to be reversed; overcrowding must be reduced; and the problem of homelessness needs to be countered. Like all major cities, Birmingham still has a housing problem. With a dynamic and proactive Housing Department this problem will be addressed as part of an integrated urban policy. Birmingham's housing history has shown the need for this approach. Its large-scale council house building was imposed from above and the views of residents were rarely sought. This top down approach has been swept away, and it is unlikely that the council will embark on any major house-building programmes in the foreseeable future. Yet the council will continue to have a crucial role in regeneration. It will carry out that role in partnership with housing associations and private enterprise. Above all, it will carry out that role in partnership with residents to provide best value in housing.

New housing on the Stockfield Estate.

Chapter 6:

Our Houses, Memories of Council Tenants and Owner Occupiers of Improved Properties

<u>The Memories of Mrs Jenkins.</u>

Interviewed by Ben Russell and Michael Harvey of Kingsland School and Nageena Suleman and Gwenhivir Moon of Oldknow School.

Mrs Jenkins grew up in a very poky house in Aston, 'just the one room downstairs, a kitchen, no garden just a little bit of a yard made with bricks . . . and two small bedrooms . . . we had a tin bath and we used to have to carry it in and keep filling the kettle up with hot water until we got enough water to have a wash and that was our bath'. The outside toilet was shared with a neighbour and 'there was no toilet rolls then we used to use newspaper.' In 1964 her home in Gladstone Street, Aston was knocked down to make way for flats and the family moved to Egerton Road, Pype Hayes where 'the pipes started rattling the first night we came. We was in bed and with the hot water coming through it made the pipes rattle and we kept turning the hot water off. 'Course we couldn't go to sleep and we realised that the more we turned it off the more they was filling up again, and all night we was up and down in bed! I mean it's laughable now, I could kick meself and I kept saying "ooh it's going again!", you know. I remember that well. We thought it was a palace when we first came although it did want doing up. But we tided it all up and had big windows put in and glass doors and made it more modern, in that way. But we thought it was a palace to the one we come out. Well it'd got a garden and everything what we wanted, you know. So it was a lot better . . . Well there was a lot of difference, for one thing we had no hot water for the little one down Aston, there was no hot water. You'd got to just light it up for the kettle and the gas stove and that's all you had and we thought it was marvellous then to turn the tap on and get some hot water and that was the main thing.' Now rehoused in Pype Hayes, she lives in a bungalow which is absolutely marvellous, 'cause it's got everything I want'.

Mrs Jenkins of Pype Hayes, April 1999.

The Memories of Irene Brown

Interviewed by Shakil Hussain of Oldknow School and Nicola Exhall and Kerry Exhall of Kingsland School.

When they married in 1948, Irene and Tom lived in a house with no water and 'we had to go to a wash house. They'd only just had the electricity put in and we had a factory next door and it used to go like the clappers. You could hear the power presses banging all day long and at night we used to have to put a cushion underneath the China Cabinet, and open it very carefully and let the glassware fall out onto . . . because everything had jogged forward. We used to keep a hand broom and a shovel on the landing, because when the power presses went the plaster used to fall off the walls, and we used to sweep that up. But Environment people, if they existed, we didn't know about. So we just had to put up with that, and we were only paying six shillings and nine pence a week for that house. Then I had the opportunity of going into one of the new flats in Nechells . . . we jumped to paying £2 and 9s (45p) a week . . . that was one big rise! and Tom kept saying "We'll never be able to afford it, we'll never be able to afford it" . . . and we moved into this flat and it was absolutely beautiful. We'd got two beautiful bedrooms, built in wardrobes, we'd got our own room to hang our washing out. We'd got central heating, and you'd never guess what I done. We spent our first night there on Saturday night. In the morning I got up and I cooked breakfast and I started to do the washing up, put the crockery into the bowl and filled the kettle up with cold water and put it on the cooker. While I'm waiting for the kettle to boil I suddenly realise I'm standing with my hand on the hot water tap. I had never ever lived in a house where there was hot water.' Nineteen years later, Irene and Tom left Queen's Tower for a new house in Aston and 'I couldn't believe that I can open the door and peg my washing out in a garden! Peg my washing out in a garden and actually speak to my neighbours over the fence!'

Tom Brown as a child on his dad's bike outside the family home in Little King Street, Hockley, 1930. Tom's dad, also Tom, is next to him.

The Memories of Gladys Vaisey

Interviewed by Asim Zaman and Shakil Hussain of Oldknow School and Nicola Exhall and Kerry Exhall of Kingsland Primary School.

Gladys Vaisey is active in the Pensioner's Convention, Neighbourhood Watch, Housing Liaison Board, a Ward Sub-Committee 'and quite a few more things'. When she was growing up her mom was a widow and 'we moved about quite a lot because she lost her house when she was in the hospital. She left the rent with my oldest sister and the lady that was the agent in the back street wanted a house for her niece so she said the sister hadn't paid her, and when me mother came home she'd been evicted. So from then on they went in a home and I was the baby so she took me round with her and we moved from place to place, but eventually when I was eighteen I got our own house, on the Lichfield Road, . . . it wasn't hard but you know poverty was existent then and if you'd got no money you didn't get any help, and if you couldn't pay your rent you were out on the street. It was as simple as that'. After her marriage, Gladys lived in Cromwell Street and when 'the daughter was ten nearly eleven, the boy was two and we got this house because they were taking them down in Nechells and I've been here forty four years ... and it's the happiest move of me life.' The removal was 'hazardous! 'cause you had to move by handcart in those days. You couldn't afford lorries and what have you. But it was great we couldn't get here quick enough. They offered me a flat to begin with and I wouldn't have that 'cause I wanted a garden for the kids. We settled in, bought bit by bit, you know what it's like my husband was on a very low salary.' The new house in Erdington had 'more room, a garden for the youngsters to play in and my husband was an avid gardener and he kept the garden beautiful as and when he could afford it and the children had their own rooms and they could get their friends in.'

Gladys Vaisey outside her council house in Erdington, April 1999.

The Memories of Dennis Sedgley

Interviewed by Shakil Hussain, Gwenhivir Moon and Nageena Suleman of Oldknow School and Michael Harvey of Kingsland School.

Dennis spent his childhood in Aston and after his marriage he and his wife lived on the Pool Farm Estate in Kings Norton before moving to a high-rise flat in Lee Bank. 'I've lived here for 31 years . . . that's when it was built 31 years ago and now they're going to knock it down in the next few months, they are. So that will be the end of this. What things have changed? When we moved in it was something out of the ordinary. Bathroom, toilet, underfloor heating. That was something we had never experienced before. We only ever went in the lift when we went to big shops in town, like Lewis's and shops like that. We never travelled in a lift before then and when we came here it was luxury. The good part was when we moved here it was something out of the ordinary. Oh it was very nice when we moved in. It was posh, we looked out the window we had a beautiful view we'd got the balcony there which you could stand and look out. Oh we used to see a lot of things . . . But over the years, when the families that first moved in and . . . they came from houses or buildings that were being demolished in other parts of the city, so it was their home, but as the years went on and they left younger people came in and they treated it as just temporary accommodation. So they didn't spend a lot of time here and people

were coming and going all the time. What's it like? It's got advantages, it's got disadvantages. The advantages is that there is only one front door, so unless someone, as regards breaking in, or burglaries they are very difficult if you are living in one and you have got a secure front door. Because they can't get in any other way they've either got to come down from the roof which is seven floors or they've got to climb up the outside which is thirteen floors, and I don't think they can do that. But it's got a beautiful view. You're utterly private, there is no one to over look you or see into here for any reason at all.'

Dennis Sedgely, 1999.

The Memories of Carlton Downes

Interviewed by Ben Russell and Michael Harvey of Kingsland School and Gwenhivir Moon and Nageena Suleman of Oldknow School.

Carlton now lives in a sheltered housing scheme for elderly people in Handsworth but he grew up in the West Indies. 'Oh yes, the house that I lived in Trinidad was beautiful! Well actually my family . . . had a big, well what we call here a bungalow but it was upstairs and downstairs . . . you know for a small island the amount of space that people have around their house is you know enormous . . . you know we had the downstairs we have living room, kitchen, things like that. Upstairs we have maybe a second living room and bedrooms and dining room and things like that. I mean this is how our house was. But you know there are other types, there are other smaller types of houses where there is just a one, well wooden house or something like that, but a galvanised roof and thing, but it's one thing that nobody has to worry about and that's heating because in Trinidad, or in the West Indies as a whole the weather is warm all the year round. So instead of trying to keep heat in we have what you call lattice wood to allow wind to blow through the house, you know so you feel cool and nice all the time.' Arriving in Birmingham in 1960, Carlton lived in Balsall Heath and 'well you know in those days housing was terrible. I lived in a bedsit actually. I don't know if you know what a bedsit is, do you? Well a bedsit is a place, it's a house that's divided up into rooms and they put a bed, a table and a chair and they rent that out. Sometimes two and three people live in one room that's not even the size of this living room. So it was really terrible in those days.' After sending for his family, Carlton moved to Sparkhill and then bought a house in Erdington. Although his first thoughts of Birmingham 'was really horrible' he has no regrets about settling here.

Carlton Downes in Trinidad.

Memories of Hassna Khatun

Interviewed by Ben Russell and Michael Harvey of Kingsland School and Gwenhivir Moon and Nageena Suleman of Oldknow School.

Hassna is a twenty-eight year old primary school teacher at Oldknow Junior School and grew up in Bangla Desh. 'I actually lived in a village, okay, and the house I lived in was actually made out of bricks and cement which was . . . supposed to mean that we were rich but I don't think that we're that rich. But anyway the village I come from was called Tandaipara and it's in a district of Syllhet . . . the house had two big rooms right and one of the rooms we actually cooked in and the other room we slept in and socialised in. It had a nice backyard, two toilets, outside. One with a roof on, one without a roof on. We also had a middle yard and another house which was also made out of cement, and that was like a guest house and a few yards down there was a big natural pool for bathing . . . the room where we all slept in it had wooden beds. We had two big wooden beds and they were like tables. There were no mattresses and . . . the whole family slept on those two beds. The floors were actually not lino but they were actually dried up mud and we didn't have any electricity, that's another thing and we actually had lanterns, oil lanterns for lighting. We had to cook on a clay stove, using wood for fuel . . . When we first came into this country we lodged with a couple of people and that was on Somerville Road and that was very cramped. We all slept in the same room. It was very, very hard for us all actually and then we moved to Kings Road, in Hay Mills and we lodged again with another family and again we had to have just one bedroom for all of us. We shared the kitchen and the living room and that was very, very hard, and then we moved to Redhill Road, where my parents live now and they actually own the house. That was the first house we owned as a whole family and it had three bedrooms a front room, a sitting room, a kitchen and a downstairs bathroom, and then I moved away to University, and now I am living in rented accommodation.

Members of Hassna Khatun's family outside their home in Syllhet, Bangla Desh, January 1994.

Hassna Khatun with some of the children she teaches at Oldknow Junior School. Hassna was responsible for the children from the school who took part in the Quest Millennium Award project.

Memories of Valerie Bloxham

Interviewed by Ben Russell and Michael Harvey of Kingsland School and Gwenhivir Moon and Nageena Suleman of Oldknow School.

Valerie is an LSA Assistant at Oldknow Junior School and grew up in Sparkbrook in a terraced house. 'We had three bedrooms and two rooms downstairs and a kitchen, but we had no bathroom. We had to have a bath in a tin bath, on a Friday night . . . the tin bath had to be brought in from the outhouse and a gas boiler was lit and filled with water and put into the bath. We had no inside toilet. The toilet was outside, so you always tried not to go out the loo in the dark and at night and there used to be spiders and I didn't like it very much and it was cold. You never went out to sit in the toilet and read a book, because it was too cold.

The house I'm living in now is in Malmesbury Road, Small Heath and I have been there for 31 years. We had a lot of alterations done because when I moved into the house that I'm in now there was a bath in the kitchen. Not fitted up with hot water taps or anything, just a bath, so we still had to heat water and fill the bath up. We could empty it away, there was a plug in it and it wasn't until about twenty years ago that we had a bathroom added on we had to have it an extension to have a bathroom on. The extension for one, that was the biggest alteration that we had done and about twelve, thirteen years ago through the Urban Renewal we had what was called an Enveloping Scheme and they came and they took the roofs off and put brand new roofs on our houses. We all had new doors and new windows so that made the area look neater and tidier. We have also had a road calming scheme put in with silent policemen, or bumps and chicanes so that's the major improvement that we have had done in the area.'

Valerie Bloxham outside Oldknow Junior School.

Valerie Bloxham during one of the interview sessions of the Quest Millennium Award funded project to get youngsters to interview older folk about their housing experiences, April 1999.

Memories of Jack Rivett

Interviewed by Ben Russell and Michael Harvey of Kingsland School and Gwenhivir Moon and Nageena Suleman of Oldknow School.

Jack was born at 23, St John's Road, Sparkhill and now lives at 91, St John's Road. Today 'lots of things have changed. Now you've got electricity, which you never had, you only had gas lighting. You've got running water in all the kitchens, you've got bathrooms, we never had bathrooms. We never had running water, we had to go across the yard to fetch the water. Well when I was at school I used to have to come home of a Monday and use the maid to maid the clothes in the tub to wash them, and you used to have to do it by hand. Then you had to take it out of the tub, take it across to the brew house and put it through the mangle, which used to squeeze all the water out of it. Then you used to have to hang it out on the line to dry. No, you didn't have any hot water you used to have to boil the water in the brew house . . . and you used to have to light a coal fire underneath the boiler to boil the water so that you got hot water. If you wanted hot water to make a cup of tea then you used to have a kettle, a

big iron kettle, hanging over the fire and that used to be boiling all the while, and that was how you used to get your hot water. The house that I live in now has had a bathroom built on by Urban Renewal, and also a toilet. It's a very good thing. It's improved the houses. It's made it better for a lot more people, and being one of the older generation I appreciate it because you don't have to suffer what we had to suffer when I was your age. Well before Urban Renewal did the alterations it was an ordinary two bedroomed house. No bathroom, no toilet. The toilet was outside, no inside toilet, and no electricity. It was all gas lighting, and coal fires and then when Urban Renewal came they turned it round, knocked the old toilet and coal house down, and built the bathroom and toilet on the back and took all the gas lighting out and put all new electricity in. So that it made it more modern. I thought I was living in a palace.'

Denise Whitehead, teaching assistant, outside Kingsland Primary School, Kingstanding, 1999. Denise was responsible for the children from the school who were involved in the Quest Millennium Award project.

Children from Kingsland and Oldknow Schools interviewing Jack Rivett, April 1999.

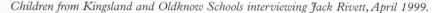

Memories of Joyce Farley

Interviewed by Asim Zaman and Shakil Hussain of Oldknow School and Nicola Exhall and Kerry Exhall of Kingsland School.

Joyce is a President of Community Forum and lived in Small Heath for 58 years. She was involved with Urban Renewal people 'at the very beginning and of course we didn't really know what Urban Renewal was. So what I did I went to the local library and I got a book out, called "Urban Renewal". Now, as far as I know the idea of urban renewal started in America. I believe the some of the City Officers, not the Councillors but the City Officers, went to see the urban renewal programme in America . . . And I went to a first meeting in . . . an old school that they had handed over to the local council because it was a bit too old to be used as a school . . . so they used part of it as an Urban Renewal Office. Now we were the first team of Urban Renewal . . . and we went to learn all about what Urban Renewal was, this was about two years before the work actually started, and they told us the sort of things they would be doing. 'Cause what you had to do you had to sign a paper to say that you'd pay so much money towards it and the rest of the money came from the Government, so you didn't get it all free, part of it was, well if you like the "free" nothing is really "free". But my mother, after I explained to her what it was all about decided that she would like to have this work done. Well, I think it could have been improved at the beginning, but it was a good scheme. The only thing is we thought it was, my organisation, Community Forum, thought it was a very slow way of doing things and we were the people that thought up the "Envelope Scheme". I think over the years Urban Renewal has been a very, very good idea. So much so that we went to Holland to see their Urban Renewal and we were very impressed and we've been to Germany to see theirs. So it's an idea that's catching on with other countries as well as, but it's had its faults. But on the whole it's been very, very good Urban Renewal. A lot of people would never have been able to afford to have their houses done up if they'd have had to pay for it themselves.'

A training day in the Department of Modern History, The University of Birmingham in which youngsters from two Birmingham schools were involved in workshop sessions to develop knowledge of the city's housing history and an awareness of interviewing techniques. The project was funded by a Quest Millennium Award after an application by Joyce Farley, President of Community Forum. Joyce is seated holding the original edition of Homes for People. *Left to right are: Asim Zaman of Oldknow School, Small Heath; Howard Pidd, Press and External Relations Manager, Birmingham City Housing Department; Kerry Exhall, Kingsland School, Kingstanding; Nageena Suleman, Oldknow School; Dr Carl Chinn, The University of Birmingham who led the training session; Michael Harvey, Kingsland School; Ben Russell, Kingsland School; Nicola Exhall, Kingsland School; Pat Muddiman, Development Officer, Birmingham City Housing Department; Gwenhivir Moon, Oldknow School; and Shakil Hussain, Oldknow School.*

Further Reading

Copies of most of the following books and unpublished manuscripts can be found in the Local Studies Department, Central Library, Birmingham. This is a treasure trove of information for anyone interested in Birmingham's history.

Working-Class Life Stories

Walter Chinn	*From Victoria's Image* (unpublished manuscript, no date)
Kathleen Dayus	*Her People* (London, 1982)
	Where There's Life (London, 1985)
	All My Days (London, 1988)
Jack Francis	*Pawnshops and Lard* (Leicester, 1989)
Syd Garrett	*I Remember ... Tales of old Ladywood* (Birmingham, no date)
Tom Golding	*96 years a Brummie* (Birmingham, 1986)
	The Brum We Knew (Birmingham, 1988)
Win Heywood	*My Mother's Story* (Northwood, 1986)
Taffy Lewis	*"Any Road". Pictures of Small Heath, Sparkbrook and further afield 1902-39* (Birmingham, 1979)
Alan Mahar (ed.)	*Memories of Balsall Heath, Highgate and Sparkbrook* (Birmingham, 1983)
	Writing It Down Before It's All Gone; working class life in Balsall Heath between the wars (Birmingham, 1984)
Leslie Mayell	*The Birmingham I Remember* (Padstow, 1980)
	Further Memories of Birmingham (Padstow, 1982)
Lily Need	*Struggling Manor. Inner City Birmingham in the 1920s* (Birmingham, 1993)
Ruth M. Slade	*Annie, Margaret, Ruth, Doreen, Nicola; A Family History* (unpublished manuscript, 1989)
Will Thorne	*My Life's Battles* (first published 1925, new edition, London, 1989)
Howard Williamson	*Toolmaking and Politics. The Life of Ted Smallbone – an oral history* (Birmingham, 1987)

Books on Working-Class Life in Birmingham

Carl Chinn	*They Worked All Their Lives: Women of the Urban Poor in England, 1880-1939* (Manchester, 1988)
Carl Chinn	*Our Brum* (Birmingham, 1997)
Carl Chinn	*Our Brum, Volume 2* (Birmingham, 1998)
Ronald K. Moore	*Up The Terrace Down Aston and Lozells* (Birmingham, 1988)
Victor Price	*Aston Remembered, Yesterday and Today (Studley, 1989)*
Pauline and Bernard	*The Summer Lane and Newtown of the Years Between The Wars 1918-1939* (Birmingham, 1985)

Novels on Working-Class Life in Birmingham

Walter Allen   *All In A Lifetime* (First published 1959, new edition, London, 1986)

John Douglas   *A Walk Down Summer Lane* (London, 1983)

Histories of Birmingham

Carl Chinn   *Birmingham: The Great Working City* (Birmingham, 1994)

Conrad Gill   *History of Birmingham Volume I. Manor and Borough to 1865* (London, 1952)

Asa Briggs   *History of Birmingham, Volume II. Borough and City 1865-1938* (London, 1952)

Anthony Sutcliffe & *History of Birmingham Volume III. Birmingham 1939-1970*
Roger Smith   (London, 1974)

Victor Skipp   *The Making of Victorian Birmingham* (Birmingham, 1983)

John Thackray Bunce *History of the Corporation of Birmingham, Volume I* (Birmingham, 1878)

John Thackray Bunce *History of the Corporation of Birmingham, Volume II* (Birmingham, 1885)

Charles Anthony Vince *History of the Corporation of Birmingham, Volumes III and IV* (Birmingham, 1902)

Joseph Trevor Jones *History of the Corporation of Birmingham, Volume V* (Birmingham, 1940)

Housing in Birmingham

Birmingham Planning *Developing Birmingham 1889-1989. 100 years of City Department Planning* (Birmingham, 1989)

Bournville Village Trust *Bournville Village Trust 1900-1955* (Birmingham, 1955)

Bournville Village Trust *When We Build Again. A Study Based on Research Into Conditions of Living and Working in Birmingham* (London, 1941)

F. Margaret Fenter *Copec Adventure. The Story of the Birmingham Copec House Improvement Society* (Birmingham, 1960)

Birmingham in Photographs

The Local Studies Department, Birmingham Central Library, contains the 'Slum Collection', an evocative collection of photographs of back-to-back houses and courtyards taken in 1904.

Michael Glasson *City Children, Birmingham Children at Work and Play 1900-1930* (Birmingham, 1985)

Dorothy McCulla   *Victorian and Edwardian Birmingham from old photographs*
                         (London, 1973)

John Whybrow and   *How Birmingham became a Great City* (Birmingham, 1976)
Rachel Waterhouse

Housing and Public Health in General

John Burnett   *A Social History of Housing 1815-1985* (2nd edition, London,
                         1986)

Carl Chinn   *Poverty amidst Prosperity. The Urban Poor in England, 1834-
                         1914* (Manchester, 1995)

Some books and articles which are mentioned in this book are not included in this list of further reading. Most can be found in Birmingham Central Library, whilst the annual reports of the city's Medical Officer of Health are in the Local Studies Department.

Where a book title is not given, then the quotes about housing by Brummies are taken from letters written to me. All my letters are in Archives, Birmingham Central Library and are available for consultation by bona fide researchers.

POSTSCRIPT TO 'HOMES FOR PEOPLE'

You can judge a city's potential by its housing. Birmingham can continue to develop as a major international city only if we support the economic vitality and the growth in the service industries with a range of housing of sufficient quality to meet the aspirations of people that want to live in the city.

Birmingham's housing stock faces a number of challenges to meet that requirement. The Council's role as landlord will change moving into the new millennium. Customer focus, empowerment of tenants and new ways of delivering social housing will all be on the agenda as we revitalise the core of social rented housing in the city. Owner occupation needs a boost. Too many owner occupied properties are deteriorating faster than they are repaired. The average house in this city will have to last for over 2,000 years at current rates of clearance. We need to find a way to improve people's homes in order to maintain the stability of the communities in which they live. Particularly around the inner-city core, the housing market requires new forms of intervention to maintain property values and to encourage investment in maintenance.

As the pressures on household growth continue so we need to find new housing markets in the city and in the area immediately around Birmingham. The City Council must work with other local authorities in the region to ensure that future housing provision within and around the city is balanced, meeting the needs of those with wealth and aspirations as well as those in poverty and deprivation. We must recapture the housing market for all tenures and price

ranges and stem the out-migration of the wealthy. Only with a mixed economy of housing will the city become truly sustainable.

These are the challenges that face us as we move into the new millennium. Good quality housing is central to sustainable communities. The City Council will continue to invest in ensuring that Birmingham has homes that meet the needs and aspirations of all of its residents and not just for the excluded minority. Investment in good quality housing is investment in the long-term future of the city. Birmingham has a great future, building on a great past.

Graham Farrant
Director of Housing

INDEX

Some sub-sections are listed in chronological order
Italics denote reference to an illustration or text appended to an illustration